Far East Buses – Volume One
Macau
The British Bus Years

~

Mike Davis
With major contributions by John Shearman

DTS
Publishing

Published by DTS Publishing Limited
PO Box 105, Croydon, Surrey.
ISBN 0 9523448 9 0

Printed by KPC Group, Ashford, Kent.

© Mike Davis 1996

British Library Cataloguing in Publication Data. A catalogue record for this book is available from the
British Library.

Contents

FRONT COVER—UPPER: Although not of Bristol manufacture, the Daimler CVG6's from Bolton were impressive vehicles. Here CV201 stands at the Taipa terminus of cross-bridge route in October 1980. (Ian Lynas

FRONT COVER—LOWER: One of Macau's 'grand old ladies', 1939 vintage Bristol L5G, once L102, waiting between duties at the leafy Barra terminus, near the southern tip of the peninsula. (Ian Lynas

FRONTISPIECE: The Dennis Darts were introduced by TRANSMAC, S.A.R.L.in January 1996— just in time for inclusion in this book. (Tim Phillips

Foreword and Acknowledgements

The author acknowledges the major and generous input of information and material by John Shearman—by far the most major contributor—and his work in checking details regarding not only individual vehicle histories but also the background to Macau and the bus operations in general.

John and I were both variously familiar with the Macau bus scene from 1973 into the early 1980s. Indeed, Shearman actually resided there, generally on a four days a week basis, from June 1974 to June 1976, during which period he was employed by the territory's major bus operator, Companhia de Auto-Carros "Fok Lei" Limitada, firstly as its consultant and then in a managerial capacity with overall responsibility for the implementation of the new policy initiatives. He therefore has in-depth personal knowledge of the Company's activities during that time. During the years 1973 to 1985—especially 1973 to 1976—observations and copious notes were made and many photographs taken. At the time of writing, late 1995, it is those references which are being used as the basis for the writing of this book. Such raw data can now only be supported by recollections, faded but believed still to be essentially accurate. Nonetheless, two decades on, it has to be recognised that whilst what is written here can be regarded as dependable, it might be that the book has shortcomings by the omission of certain details which ought otherwise to have been included. The problem with memory failure is that one does not even know what information, however relevant, has been forgotten!

The book should thus be read and interpreted with it firmly borne in mind that it takes as its foundation the situation and activities relating to Macau's buses as they were in the mid-1970s. From that starting point the book endeavours to work both backwards and forwards in time but, of necessity, the emphasis has had to remain centred on the years 1973 to 1977. Fortunately, however, that coincides with the era in which the interest provided by the deployment of second-hand buses from the United Kingdom peaked.

Pre-1973 information was given verbally to Shearman during the 1974 to 1976 period by Mr. Chen Cheong Kei, manager of "Fok Lei" since the mid or late 1950s, and by Mr. Ho Kun Meng, an administrator within the Company and whose father had been a bus driver for them since the early post-war years.

Fortunately both Mr. Chen and Mr. Ho with their excellent commands of spoken English were able to impart their first hand knowledge with ease. Sincere thanks are owed to them both for their patience in answering historical questions the nature of which must have seemed rather odd to Chinese gentlemen whose culture did not embrace bus enthusiasm other than for the economical and dependable operational characteristics of Gardner engined Bristols.

Information from 1977 onwards is derived almost exclusively from our separate subsequent but only occasional and brief visits to Macau until 1985 and from the visitations of many enthusiasts to the territory since the mid-1970s to see the British buses operating there. By then many of the buses were increasingly deserving of the title 'truly vintage' and were amongst the world's oldest surviving buses still in all-day regular service.

It seems that, with the exception of an acquaintance of Mr. F. W. York, who, in 1953—prior to the arrival of the first second-hand buses from the UK—briefly called-in at Macau in order to take photographs at the latter's request—and another in 1966 who photographed some Bristol L5G's, few bus enthusiasts even realised that Macau was a Mecca for Bristol L and LS buses and Beadle-Bedford chassisless buses exiled from the British Transport Commission, let alone visited the place before 1973 to see them. If any reader did do so then we appeal to him, please, to contact the publisher so that whatever supplementary historical information and/or photographs which he may be able to supply can published or studied for data.

Although John Shearman has been the major contributor, I must also thank Maurice Doggett for some last minute research, as well as Alan Townsin and Ron Phillips. Danny Chan provided some late details to complete the modern vehicle data. Tim Phillips and Shirrie Chan worked hard to collect information about the present day bus companies in Macau and provided the Chinese characters where appropriate. In Macau, details of their companies were kindly supplied by Ms Chan Hio Ieong 陳曉陽小姐 of Transmac and Mr. Au Chung Kwong 區重光先生, Manager of TCM.

The photographers have been acknowledged beneath each illustration but, if we have got it wrong, we apologise but, please, contact the publishers.

NOTE: The English language spelling for Macau is *'Macao'* but this is outdated and now rarely used. It is thus appropriate and proper to select the Portuguese spelling with a 'u' for this book. The Chinese name for Macau when spoken is *'Ou Mun'* but this is only ever seen written in Chinese characters. Macau's name is derived from the Chinese, *'A-manga'* or 'Bay of the Goddess A-ma'—'A-ma' being the goddess of sailors

Introduction to Macau

Geographical Location

Macau is a small peninsula on the southern coastline of China and is physically attached to the Chinese Province of Guangdong (Kwangtung). It is situated on the west bank of the Pearl River estuary overlooking the South China Sea. Upstream is the city of Guangzhou (Canton) which lies about 87 miles (140km) north of Macau. Across the estuary, some 40 miles (64km) eastwards, lies Hong Kong.

Geographical Composition and Area

During the 1970's, that is before recent extensive reclamations, the Portuguese Overseas Province of Macau had a total area of approximately 6.5 square miles (17sq km). Compare that with the 400 square miles (1036 sq km) of then contemporary Hong Kong.

Macau is comprised of three readily definable parts:

Principally there is the Macau peninsula, joined by an isthmus to the Chinese mainland. Its area is 2.4 square miles (6.21 sq km), with a north-south length of 2.5 miles (4.1km) and a maximum width across about 1 miles (1.6km).

South of the peninsula lies the offshore island of Taipa. This was 2 miles (3.2km) long—before the addition of the airport— and 1 mile (1.6km) wide, with an area of 1.5 square miles (3.8sq km) and is of a fairly regular oval shape.

South again is Coloane, another offshore island. This is of less regular shape, 3 miles long(4.8km) with a maximum width of 1 miles (1.6km), and an area of 2.7 square miles (7sq km).

In recent years, both the peninsula and the islands have been extended in area by substantial reclamation, greatly adding to the above dimensions so that the total area of the enclave is now approximately 9sq miles (26sq km).

Off-shore to the east of Taipa—and connected to it by two causeways—is the artificial island that forms the runway of the international airport completed in 1995. The two connecting causeways form taxiways to the terminal located on reclaimed land at the east end of Taipa.

Reclamation on the peninsula is less spectacular only in not having the glamour of an international airport and the extensive new area extending into the sea from the south side of Avenida da Amizade is 700 metres east-west by 350 metres north-south—almost a quarter of a million square metres. Another, slightly larger area has been reclaimed from a small harbour on the north-east 'shoulder' of the peninsula, immediately north of the reservoir

These areas of land reclamation won from the estuary/sea add to the impression of mostly flat terrain as traversed by most roads, especially those which support bus services. However, all three parts of Macau do have very distinct hills.

History, Political Status, Trade, Rule of the Road

Macau's history as a Portuguese territory is a long one, pre-dating nearby Hong Kong's as a British Crown Colony by nearly three centuries. The Chinese Emperor in 1557 gifted the peninsula to the Portuguese Kingdom as a reward for the latter's assistance in tackling coastal piracy. Later two offshore islands were added.

Thus, by 1841, when the British established Hong Kong the Portuguese were already 'old China hands' in Macau. During the Pacific War (1941-1945) Macau remained neutral by virtue of Portugal's wartime neutrality whilst all around in China and Hong Kong the Japanese were in occupation. However this did leave Macau isolated and barely independent of Japan's will and determination.

Since the 1949 communist take-over in China that country's exertions over Macau have been increasingly felt. This culminated in the Cultural Revolution of the late 1960's causing the Portuguese to define the Territory as Chinese albeit administered by Portugal. Later the Portuguese indicated their willingness to withdraw in the aftermath of their revolution of 1974 when decolonisation became their policy but this offer was discreetly ignored by Beijing (Peking) probably so as not to cause a ripple effect which could have destabilised economic confidence in Hong Kong. However, consequent upon the Joint Declaration of 1984 by which sovereignty of Hong Kong will be returned to China by Britain with effect from 1st July 1997 it became inevitable that Portugal and China would follow suit with a similar agreement for Macau. Thus it is that Macau will revert to Chinese sovereignty on 20th December 1999.

Macau is governed by a Lisbon-appointed governor and cabinet, with a legislative council of appointed and elected local representatives. The City is presided over by a Mayor from the Leal Senado[1] building and each island has its own island council.

Macau's economy is based on the manufacturing of such goods as garments and toys but relies heavily on the revenue generated by the vast gambling industry.

The currency of Macau is the Macau Pataca, of a few cents less value than the Hong Kong dollar—which circulates freely with the Pataca—and fully convertible. The common written form uses the dollar $-sign, prefixed with an M, thus: M$

Although Macau has no British connections whatsoever, its economy and trade have long been closely linked to that of the much larger Hong Kong. Such a situation was emphasised during the years when Mao Tse Tung had 'closed' China. Nevertheless Macau's border with China never became so much of a divide as did Hong Kong's border with China. Now all the area's borders are very much 'open'.

---

[1] FOOTNOTE: 'LEAL SENADO' TRANSLATES FROM PORTUGUESE INTO ENGLISH AS THE 'LOYAL SENATE'. IT HAS THE ADMINISTRATIVE FUNCTION EQUIVALENT TO BEING MACAU CITY'S LOCAL GOVERNMENT.

Obvious and readily visible manifestations of Macau's economic ties with Hong Kong are vehicular and the rule of the road. Most vehicles delivered to Macau are supplied by Hong Kong's importing agents as an extension of their own market. In consequence British manufacturers dominated Macau's car, lorry and bus intake during the 'fifties and 'sixties and until Japanese vehicles swamped both territo-ries. Furthermore, like Hong Kong, Macau continues to drive on the left. But then so does Japan. However, in this context it is relevant to remember that Portugal itself drove on the left until 1928 and that China did likewise until 1946. The persistence of this rule made second-hand buses from the UK readily useable in Macau without there being any need to cut new doorways into the other side of the bodies.

Matters Demographic

While Chinese is the lingua franca, the Portuguese language has legal standing and English is often used as the commercial and touristic language.

Macau's people are, of course, almost all ethnically Chinese, with only a sprinkling of Portuguese and mixed-race Eurasian Macanese. Very few persons indeed of other nationalities or races reside there.

The mid-1970's population was some 300,000. The vast majority live and work on the peninsula which is almost entirely urbanised with the ever growing numbers of ever taller multi-storey blocks increasingly dominating at the expense of low-rise buildings of traditional Portuguese or South China architecture. This urbanisation extends almost to the Chinese border, although there was a 'closed area', this having been a narrow strip for security reasons. The high population density provides for an excellent bus operating environment, at least in terms of passenger loadings and service frequencies, if not in terms of congestion, fare levels, etc.

Both Taipa and Coloane Islands were completely rural, with each having only one village and but few other scattered dwellings, although Coloane also had a cluster of these at Ka Ho which could have been described as a hamlet until recently; it now faces the runway of the newly opened international airport, described briefly below, so its peace is now shattered by the roar of big jets.

However, of late, Taipa is being rapidly developed in a variety of ways, whilst Coloane has been regarded as better suited for continuing agriculture and as a recreational zone—including a golf course—for outdoor pursuits, and is notable for its attractive Hac Sa Beach.

External Transport

The normal route for virtually all travellers to arrive at, and depart from, Macau is by sea across the Pearl River Estuary from and to Hong Kong and it is anticipated that this will remain the case for many years, despite the recent opening of the new airport. In the early 1970's this was possible either by a fleet of three ships, or by hydrofoils operated by two separate companies. By the late 1970's jetfoils had speeded—and smoothed—the crossing, to be joined in due course by hovercraft operated by Hong Kong Ferries—formerly the Hongkong and Yaumati Ferry Company—and later by a variety of jet powered catamarans and high speed ferries. Other services include a river-boat to Canton (Guangzhou) plying the Pearl River.

A much more obscure arrival by sea could have been made until 1974 by the small ship—named the 'Dili'—which plied between Portuguese Macau and Portuguese Timor. Sailings were infrequent, possibly monthly, and,

Macau's Registration Number System

In overall appearance, the registration number plates are the same as those used in Portugal prior to 1992. The letters and numbers replicate the size and style of such Portuguese plates and, likewise, they are white on a black background. The similarity extends to there being a hyphen between the prefix letter, or letters, and the first pair of numerals and then another hyphen between the first and second pairs of numerals.

The very few available 1950's photographs of buses show them still to be carrying registrations in the original series which it is supposed commenced at M.1—note the dot, not a hyphen.

At some date, probably in the late 1950's, it would seem that one thousand was added to all numbers so that M.1—if it still survived—would have become M-10-01 and, for example, "Fok Lei's" number M.86, would have been changed to M-10-86. It is thought that M-99-99 was reached circa 1977 at which time the M-00-01 to M-10-00 series was commenced. (One reference book implies, wrongly, that the M-00-01 to M-10-00 series was issued before the M-10-01 to M-99-99 series.)

With the single letter M series exhausted circa 1978, Macau adopted the MA-00-01 to MA-99-99 series, followed by MB, MC, MD, et seq series.

It is important to note that, when a vehicle was scrapped, sometimes, if not always, its registration number was re-issued and this procedure certainly involved some of "Fok Lei's" vehicles, eg some of the later Bristol LS5G's were given previously issued—and hence early—numbers.

Of even greater importance for those persons concerned with identifying individual vehicles and tracing their progress over the years within the "Fok Lei" fleet is for them to be ever aware of the not infrequent occurrence of registration number swapping within a group of vehicles, notably but not exclusively, affecting the Bristol L5G's. Swapping, or donating, of numbers even occurred—but less frequently—between different vehicle types but, of course, this was much more obvious to the observer.

It has to be said that this has deceived more than one incautious vehicle photographer/recorder with the result that certain buses (again mostly Bristol L5G's) have had their chassis identity assumed—but wrongly so—by all-too-easy reference to their current registration numbers. This problem of correctly identifying individual vehicles, particularly difficult since 1976, and the unfortunate effect it has had in maintaining and publishing accurate fleet records for "Fok Lei" is elaborated upon as and where necessary in the following text and vehicle lists. The situation is incapable now of being fully resolved.

of course, ceased after the Portuguese left East Timor soon after the revolution in Portugal.

Macau's debut on the stage of world aviation is reported to have come in 1937—on 29th April to be precise—when the first scheduled flight from the USA to the mainland of Asia landed on the waters of the Outer Harbour. The term scheduled was by default, however, as it was planned for the 'Pan Am' flying boat concerned to make the nearby British colony of Hong Kong its destination. Reports suggest that the British authorities had bowed to pressure from its Imperial Airways who hoped to make Hong Kong its exclusive gateway to China. Soon after Pan Am's first flight had landed, it seems, the British relented and the 'Hong Kong Clipper' flew-on the 40-miles to the British colony and Macau bowed out of the aviation limelight—for a while.

Soon after the Pacific War ended there had been a sea-

It was to be a further thirty-one years before Macau was to take its place as a player on the world's air transport map—until 1995 in fact—when the territory's first airport was completed alongside Taipa Island. Although not officially opened at the time, the first landing by a Boeing 747 took place in November 1995 when a Cathay Pacific freighter delivered racing cars for the Macau Grand Prix, an annual motor race on a street circuit of great local and Asian prestige.

In the meantime, helicoptors have, from time to time, been used to bring the joys of big-time gambling closer to those Hong Kong businessmen whose dollars swell the coffers of the Macau Government. A current helicopter service has been running successfully for about five years.

The territory has never been rail connected although, apparently, about a hundred years ago definite proposals were made and planning initiated for a Canton to Macau

ABOVE: The traditional means of travel between Macau and Hong Kong had, until the 1960's, been by ferry but the advent of the faster hydrofoils and—later—Jetfoils sounded their death knell until only the less well off and tourists in search of a leisurely 3¹/₂ hour cruise used them for day travel. Cabins made them a little more attractive for night travel, when the hydrofoils were unable to operate. Here the *'Nam Shan'* is under way in the Pearl River estuary, bound for Hong Kong in 1975

LEFT: During the 1970's, the *hidroplanadores*—hydrofoil—had become established. Their journey-time of 75-minutes was far more attractive to those in a hurry to reach the gambling tables in Macau's casinos but the crossing was later further reduced to 45 minutes when the Boeing Jetfoils were introduced about 1975. Here the 'Flying Flamingo' 'flies' into Macau's outer harbour on arrival from Hong Kong. *(Mike Davis*

plane service between Hong Kong and Macau, using a Catalina flying boat, which earned infamy as it suffered the world's first-ever aerial hi-jack, the motive being provided by its cargo of gold bullion.

During 1961, the Macau Air Transport Company Ltd. commenced a service four times daily between Hong Kong and Macau. The Company operated for about three years but had faded from the scene by the end of 1964. During the company's brief presence, a Piaggio P136 amphibian was operated, at Hong Kong using the Kai Tak runway and at Macau using the waters of the outer harbour. (The author believes that the 'plane may have been wrecked during Typhoon Ida in October 1964.)

line. New plans were made public late in 1995 for a rail connection with China, entering Macau by way of a bridge to Taipa from an adjacent Chinese island.

The road through Macau's 'Portas do Cerco' or, in English, Barrier Gate—a decorative masonry archway—into China remained open in a very restricted way after Mao Tse Tung's communist take-over of China. In the 1973-76 period, this limited traffic appeared to comprise Chinese registered/owned vehicles only, entirely lorries—apart from a bus service using left-hand drive Chinese-built 'midibuses' (although the term 'midibus' had not been coined at the time) but non-Chinese were not normally permitted to use this service. In keeping with our main British buses theme, it is of interest that Commer minibuses were also operated by the Chinese carrier, believed to have been Kee Kwan, named after the hamlet that forms the border post on the China side of the border, now part of Gongbei. It is believed that Macau vehicles did not enter China—at least after 1949—until relatively recently.

Today, buses and coaches, both scheduled and charter tour vehicles, run into and out of China at frequent intervals every day, many joining-up with similar services from Hong Kong at terminal points in Guangzhou (Canton).

Internal Transport

The territory has prolific bus services. Taxis are readily available and so too were three-wheeled pedal trishaws. Increasingly the latter became used for leisurely recreational jaunts rather than for serious transport; now the few that remain are for tourists to 'experience' on very short trips. Traffic overall is considerable, with Macau being one of several claimants for having the world's highest traffic density. In addition to private cars, motor-cycles are popular as distances are short whilst lorries and vans are widely used for local distribution.

There was in operation a passenger—not-vehicular—ferry service at one time providing the only links to the two islands. The two vessels operated a service from a landing stage at Barra—near the southernmost point of the penin-

sula—to Taipa and on to Coloane. The Taipa pier was remote from Taipa's village—the connection being made by shuttle-bus—but Coloane's pier was located at its village. The opening of the causeway, perhaps not surprisingly, did not result in the curtailment of the Taipa-Coloane stage of the ferry service, but it was something of a surprise that the later opening of the first bridge did not cause the immediate withdrawal of the ferry service. For a while it struggled to compete against the new cross-bridge bus services but soon succumbed.

Presumably the few vehicles on Taipa and Coloane Islands prior to the advent of the bridge were delivered to the islands by means of coastal lighters (barges) on an individually contracted basis.

LEFT: The ricksha—or rickshaw—was once a common form of transport throughout Asia, until public social conscience in respect of man-powered transport prevailed. In many places, however, pedal-powered trishaws replaced the traditional pullers, marginally more acceptable in some eyes, but the effect was the same; cheap fares kept bus fares down. Here the competition of trishaw and Bristol LS bus make their way across *Rua da Praia Grande* into *Avineda de Almeida Riberio* in March 1975. *(Mike Davis*

The Causeway

During the late 1960's, an impressive causeway, straight throughout and over a mile (1,6km) in length, was opened for vehicular and pedestrian traffic to link together Taipa and Coloane Islands. Until a road bridge was opened in 1974, this causeway carried very little traffic indeed as the islands supported few vehicles with most of the limited road network on both islands being unsealed.

It is not known to the author why the causeway was built to join two truly rural islands before the bridge linked Taipa to

the Macau peninsula - certainly from the traffic and economic development viewpoints the islands' causeway, without the connecting bridge to the city to generate traffic, appeared to achieve little for some years.

One really would suppose that the logical sequence of events would have been firstly to link Taipa to Macau with the bridge, and secondly to extend the bridge's role by then linking Taipa to Coloane with the causeway. Instead, this construction schedule was reversed.

The Bridges

On 5th October 1974 the entire geographical nature of Macau changed. That morning the territory seemed as if it had enlarged itself by a factor of three! The Macau-Taipa bridge—intended to have been named 'Ponte Nobre de Carvalho', after General Nobre de Carvalho, the Governor who opened it—was at last opened to traffic. It was a huge engineering feat of which Portugal and 'little' Macau could be most justifiably proud.

All of a sudden the frustrated and constrained drivers of small and congested Macau City, who were not permitted to enter China, could motor to the open and rural roads of Taipa, and then on, via the causeway, to the equally uncongested roads of Coloane. In the reverse direction the few countryside drivers of the islands could suddenly dare to venture into the turmoil of the city's roads, whereas previously they had hardly ever seen the tail light of a vehicle ahead of them.

The bridge is straight and has a length of approximately 1.5 miles miles (3.36km) and for a considerable distance from each end it runs level, not many feet above the surface of the shallow water; it then rises as it approaches the shipping lane, near its centre, to a height sufficient to allow coastal shipping to pass beneath. It has sidewalks for pedestrians on both sides of the carriageway and the plethora of high, closely spaced, lamp standards which rise along its western side make an impressive sight when viewed at an oblique angle—especially at night.

bus operation and the bus operators throughout the territory, about which much more is said later.

Second Bridge

A second bridge, sometimes referred to as the 'Friendship Bridge' or, in Portuguese, 'Ponte de Amizade', was opened during the summer of 1995 in preparation for the additional traffic expected to arise as a result of the opening of the airport on Taipa later that year.

The Macau to Taipa bridge, seen from the Macau end, looking towards Taipa. The raised centre portion is to clear the shipping lane to Macau's Inner Harbour and neighbouring Chinese islands. *(Mike Davis*

Initially, there was a toll payable to cross the bridge, the booths being located at the Taipa end. After a while (perhaps a year) the bridge became free to cross, just as the causeway had always been.

At the time of the bridge opening, much of the crash programme to tarmac the islands' roads remained unfinished but this work proceeded at an urgent pace—although it still had not been fully completed at the time double-deck bus operation commenced, so, for a while, there was the spectacle of such buses kicking-up the dust on dirt roads.

The bridge had a dramatic effect in many respects on

This second fixed crossing leaves the peninsula at a point on the eastern edge of the reservoir and also east of the jetfoil and catamaran piers in the Outer Harbour, which were themselves relocated a short distance eastwards to make way for the massive reclamation in the area. The bridge runs out at low level over the shallow waters, then rises to cross the line of the maritime channel taken by the jetfoils. It returns to low level before again rising to clear the main shipping channel and then making a low level landfall on the east side of Taipa Island near the new Pac On Industrial Estate from where new roads connect it to the new airport terminal.

BELOW: A commercial postcard showing two interesting buses; that nearer the camera being similar to that on the left and above and the other showing a rear destination box in use—showing route 4—by a post-war BBW bodied Bristol L5G and is probably the former HAE 12, chassis 50.073. *(John Shearman collection*

The Bus Operators
1—Macau Peninsula/City

Pre-Pacific War Years

Little historical information concerning Macau's buses and their operations prior to the Pacific War is available to the author. It is understood that the vehicles were 'lorry-buses', and were operated by a number of small companies, there being perhaps as many as thirteen such owner-operators, some of whom only owned a single vehicle.

Wartime

The Pacific War more directly affected Macau from December 1941, following the fall of Hong Kong, although Japan had been attacking China since 1937. By mid-1942, Japan had occupied all the surrounding territories, including adjacent areas of South China, Hong Kong and the islands and waters of the Pacific Ocean, including the South China Sea. Macau itself, as a Portuguese Overseas Province, remained neutral and unoccupied although supplies normally obtained from, or via, China or Hong Kong became scarce and soon fuel and spares became completely unobtainable so that operation of buses in Macau ceased until the return of peace.

Immediate Post-War Years

Information on this era is also scant, but we are advised that four bus operators emerged soon after the war, probably in 1946, and once again used 'lorry-buses'. At least one of these companies, the name of which translates into "The Public Bus Company" is believed to have been a pre-war operator. It built, or had built for it, proper bus bodies on World War II Canadian Ford military truck chassis. However, reportedly it went out of business following a strike but was taken over by a Mr. Ho Yin who re-formed it to become "Companhia de Auto-Carros "Fok Lei" Limitada." At about the same time the other operators either ceased to trade or were taken over by "Fok Lei", thereby giving the new company a monopoly.

Companhia de Auto-Carros "Fok Lei" Limitada, Macau.

"Fok Lei", when translated from Chinese into English implies the concept of 'public service' or 'public utility'.

"Fok Lei", to which the Company's name was popularly abbreviated, was probably formed in 1952, and took over the operations and vehicles of all then existing bus operators. This included the approximately fifteen Canadian Fords of the "Public Bus Company", referred to above. The 'lorry buses' once owned by the other three companies were soon discarded.

The Company, in possession of its exclusive franchise awarded by the Leal Senado to operate all scheduled bus services on the peninsula, thus became Macau's firmly established bus operator. As such it was able steadily to expand its fleet and route operations necessary to meet the needs of a fast growing population. Even so, its franchise was subject to periodic renewal.

It has to be said that the strength of position enjoyed by "Fok Lei" was greatly aided by the importance of its proprietor, the late Mr. Ho Yin, who was one of Macau's most prominent and influential businessmen with wide-ranging interests, and he enjoyed the unofficial, but vital, political support of the Authorities across the border in the People's Republic of China.

With its monopolistic franchise, with the local influence of its owner and with political support from Canton (Guangzhou), "Fok Lei" had an unchallenged position. Indeed, even the trade union to which its employees belonged was, in effect, a local branch of a workers' association based in Canton. This combination of factors enabled "Fok Lei" to serve the travelling public of Macau well and successfully throughout the fifties and sixties with a fleet of conventional single-decker buses which had grown to number almost fifty by 1974. Five urban routes were in operation, covering most of the city. However, in the early 1970's, complaints about its performance were beginning to be expressed whilst, as a company, it also had its (legitimate) grievances and serious problem areas such that by 1974 matters which could have threatened the continued existence of "Fok Lei" were coming to a head.

Thus it was that in July 1974 "Fok Lei" engaged its consultant who proceeded to present it with a steady flow of new strategies for consideration and possible adoption. In the event, the multifarious recommendations made to it were almost all immediately accepted by the Company, and those which were of public concern were then further endorsed by the 'Leal Senado'. The suggested strategies were thus promptly absorbed by the Company so that the task then became one of actually implementing the new and/or amended policies. Their implementation was recognised to be a matter of urgency, and so it was proposed that the new schemes all be in place within two years, a tight and demanding schedule. The programme then proceeded so very rapidly that innovation had already commenced as early as October 1974, and continued at a pace such that by mid-1976 virtually all (but with two very frustrating exceptions—no one-man-operation and no double-decks on city routes) of the policy objectives had either been successfully—and profitably—achieved ahead of target, or were well on course for early realisation—i.e. the new depot and workshops, on a site then located within the (then) 'closed area', near the frontier, mentioned earlier.

The result of all this hectic, but relatively low cost, activity was a highly visible and significant transformation in "Fok Lei"'s character, public presentation and 'modus operandi'. It all contributed to enabling the Company to expand and to survive for about another one and half decades until the territory's bus operating structure and ownership regime was totally reorganised.

Several of the tasks and changes introduced by "Fok Lei" were of an internal management nature regarding such matters as the overall economics of its bus operation, finances and administration, details of scheduling, employees' working environments, the fare structure, etc., or were related to the complex negotiations necessary to secure the renewal of its franchise and so are unlikely to be of any particular concern to the majority readership of this book. Hence those matters will be passed over here.

However, most of the more obvious and high-profile initiatives made by "Fok Lei" during the 1974–1976 era *do* interest students of British buses operating overseas, notably:

- the introduction of double-decker buses to Macau, including:
- the region's first open-toppers—it was several years before Hong Kong and Manila copied this piece of enterprise;
- the extensive rehabilitation, rebodying even, of many of the elderly half-cab Bristol single-deckers;
- the purchase of new Albions;
- the introduction of new bus routes across the spectacular bridge;
- the new depot and workshops which enabled major rebuilds on vehicles to proceed;
- the move to an on-board-bus one-way passenger-

flow system on single-deckers involving a front-entrance/centre-exit/seated conductress and replacement of swing gates by power doors (these features were intended as first steps toward eventual one-man-operation);

- the application of a new livery the basic inspiration for which, it is openly acknowledged, was the brightness of the yellow and cream of Newcastle's erstwhile trolleybuses and Alexander Northern's buses—although Portuguese eyes may see it as reminiscent of the Coimbra livery, albeit without the grey!

It was also at this time that "Fok Lei" officially adopted an additional name for itself,'Macau Bus Service', but which, being in the English language, had no legal status. It was, however, added to itsd headed paper and incorporated into an emblem that was applied to some newly acquired and rehabilitated buses.

2—Islands (pre-Bridge)

The origins of bus operation on Macau's two off-shore islands are not known to either the author or his correspondents.

Prior to the building of the causeway which linked the two islands, it is probable that there was already a bus service of sorts connecting the remote Taipa ferry pier to Taipa village whilst a bus service was less likely on Coloane as the ferry pier was located within that island's village. However, there might already have been some kind of very occasional public transport from Coloane village to Ka Ho.

In 1970, or thereabouts, the causeway opened and, either at that time, or at some time later, a bus service commenced operation over it to link Taipa village with Coloane village. The causeway itself was this route's only section of sealed road, other than short sections within the confines of the two villages.

July 1973 to October 1974

When, in July 1973, John Shearman made an initial visit to the islands, the situation which greeted him was one of a fascinating collection of elderly and odd buses, lorry-buses and a minibus, all with British manufactured chassis, in various states of operation, repair or dereliction; distinctions not always entirely obvious! There were also a number of poorly maintained cars in use as taxis.

Each island had its own separate bus company.

Taipa

The green and cream buses of Taipa proclaimed the operator's name to be variously 'COMPANHIA DE AUTO-OMNIBUS DA TAIPA' or just 'AUTO-OMNIBUS DA TAIPA' which was boldly painted in white lettering along the

sides of certain of its vehicles, together with the equivalent in Chinese script below the Portuguese—the Chinese script being in a larger size than that of the Portuguese. Ferry arrivals and departures at Taipa pier were met and buses transported passengers to and from the village. This service was the nearest that either island then had in the way of a regular and dependable bus service but, even then, there were only a few journeys each day.

Coloane

The crimson and cream buses of the Coloane Island's bus company boasted the fleet name LO WAN LEE ON— 路環利安巴士公司 —only in Chinese. An occasional service operated from the village over a well surfaced road as far as Hac Sa but which then continued along the remote and rough tracks to just beyond the hamlet of Ka Ho using, one supposes, either a 'lorry-bus' or a minibus to work this service.

Another occasional bus service was operated via the causeway to link Taipa and Coloane villages (although the islands remained linked by the passenger ferry) and buses of both operators were noted working this route from time to time. However, to describe it as a jointly operated route would imply a degree of sophisticated working arrangements hardly required for such an infrequent service.

Nonetheless, without this causeway bus route, it seemed that Coloane's buses would have had virtually no purpose. As it was, only the recreational visits of city dwellers at weekends caused the buses of either island to see much use, those of Coloane in particular being otherwise mostly idle. In contrast, certain summer Sunday journeys could, therefore, be very busy, catering for trippers.

3—Cross Bridge and Islands

CTPEMI—including island local routes

The months before the October 1974 opening of the bridge which connects Macau City to Taipa—and which was to have such an ever expanding effect on both islands—caught both of the island bus operators entirely unprepared for the total change in operating environment which was imminent. Neither had given any consideration to the huge new opportunities which were before them

for new bus services across the bridge, nor had they thought to cater for the new travel demands within the islands that the influx of visitors from the city could be expected to create.

The first move, a couple of months before the bridge opening date, was an approach by "Fok Lei" to both operators to acquire them outright as that Company had started in July 1974 to make its own plans to introduce cross-bridge routes (this itself being an overdue start to planning) immediately upon the bridge being declared open.

These negotiations came to nothing, not being well received by the Islands' Council which was not particularly inclined to see the city bus operator's monopoly sphere extended to embrace the rural islands.

On the other hand, it was obvious that neither of the local bus operators had the corporate capacity necessary to expand themselves at such a late stage to cope with the demands which the bridge would inevitably impose upon them; but something had to be done, and quickly.

Thus it was that the entrepreneurial interests which were operating the soon to be challenged ferry service entered the impasse shortly before the bridge opened by duly acquiring both of the islands' bus operators and, from that nucleus, a new bus company was immediately formed, namely 'COMPANHIA DE TRANSPORTE DE PASSAGERIOS ENTRE MACAU E ILHAS LIMITADA' (CTPEMI).

ABOVE: So hard pressed were CTPEMI on the first weekend of cross-bridge operations, that they were forced to resort to running Bedford SB5's so new that they were not yet registered and ran in service on the local equivalent of British 'Trade Plates' as this crowded example illustrates. It was one of the first two of the type. *(John Shearman*

With only a matter of a few weeks remaining, there were now two operators—"Fok Lei" and CTPEMI—wanting to operate buses across the bridge but with no agreements or arrangements in place. "Fok Lei" had no operating rights on the islands, CTPEMI had none in the city. There was thus no alternative but to negotiate joint operation for cross-bridge bus services, enabling one to penetrate the other's monopoly area. But the less than harmonious relationship between the two business interests necessitated the good offices of, principally, the 'Leal Senado' but also of the Islands' Council to ensure that a satisfactory operating agreement between the two operators was achieved before the authorities could franchise the proposed services.

In the event, on behalf of both operators, it was "Fok Lei" which actually devised the three new bus services which were to be introduced and produced the overall timetable which was to be worked on a 50/50 basis but without any pooling of revenue between operators. The basic arrangement was for alternate journeys on each of the routes, to be worked by each operator. The fares were agreed amongst all concerned parties, *ie*, both operators and both councils, whilst the Government set the bridge toll charges from which public buses were not exempt.

Although the raison d'etre for CTPEMI's formation was to share in the forthcoming cross-bridge bus services, in the process of achieving that objective it had had to inherit the local bus services on Taipa and Coloane and the local route connecting those two islands. As such, CTPEMI had become the monopoly operator for all bus services within the two islands and although it regarded such a privilege to be secondary, it had to content itself with performing only this relatively minor role for the short while between the Company's formation and the opening of the bridge.

Initially, to operate its local routes, CTPEMI used a few buses selected from the motley collection which it had acquired with the two local bus companies. This, however, was to be only a short term expedient as new replacement vehicles, in the shape of Bedford SB5's, were hurriedly ordered the delivery of which had to be treated as a matter of urgency by the Hong Kong-based supplying agent.

However, this new ordering was not intended for the small scale intra-island operation but was instead to provide CTPEMI with the fleet of vehicles it would need to operate its fifty percent share of the much more important cross bridge bus routes. This fleet steadily grew in order to accommodate the rapidly expanding patronage on these routes.

"Fok Lei"

"Fok Lei" viewed the inauguration of the cross-bridge bus services as an opportunity to make a small beginning towards the introduction of the first of its planned new operating methods which it was intended would gradually be extended to its established network of city routes. Because of the short lead time available for planning and implementation—only from about late July to early October—it was not possible that these innovations could be many by day-one of the bridge services but at least the three Bristol L5G's (*qv*) initially allocated to the bridge services were newly overhauled, two of which introduced the bright new yellow livery to the streets and had been converted to the newly devised passenger-flow/seated conductress layout but still with swing gates.

Additional vehicles had also been ordered by "Fok Lei" to enable it adequately to meet its fifty per cent commitment to the routes. These were two new single-deckers, delivery of which was to be rushed ahead of Albion's build programme by diverting chassis which had been destined for delivery to the Kowloon Motor Bus Co. in Hong Kong. However, it was not intended that these two buses would be allocated for very long to the bridge routes as the substantive plan was to operate these high profile routes exclusively with a dedicated fleet of double-deck buses and to do so on a permanent basis. Never before had such large buses been operated in Macau. These had, of necessity, to be second-hand for reasons of cost and because, in any case, traditional front-engined models which were wanted in order to retain engineering simplicity within the fleet, were no longer being manufactured other than by Ashok-Leyland,

service. Initially four were available, three being required to operate "Fok Lei's" fifty per cent share of routes 11 and 21 (although at weekends route 21A required the fourth). It was a notable event, widely welcomed, and over the ensuing years the double-deckers, whose total grew to eleven, were most successfully operated on all three of the original cross-bridge services where their high capacity was often an essential requirement. As

LEFT: Immdeiately prior to the official opening of the Bridge on 5th October 1974, "Fok Lei" placed its inaugural vehicle strtagically on the level section. Here Bristol L128 (M-11-47) awaits the first public passenger journey 'across the water' in the company of LS139 which was used as a 'support car'. *(John Shearman.*

in India. (Guy Victory and Dennis Jubilant double-deckers are front engined but not of traditional design and had yet to make their appearance in Hong Kong.)

Unfortunately, not only did it take a few months to locate suitable double-deckers in the United Kingdom— it was a time of an acute scarcity of supply; so much so that the situation was the subject of an article in the 'Commercial Motor' issue of 15th November 1974— but also extensive programmes of raising overhanging illuminated advertisement boards in the city and tree lopping on the two islands had to take place before double-deck operation could be introduced to the territory. That took longer still and so it was not until Monday 16th June 1975 that Macau's first double-deckers entered

second-hand buses, cheap to buy and remaining unrebodied, they gave long and creditable service to Macau—although not to be compared to the longevity which "Fok Lei" coaxed from their L5G chassis!

The jointly operated cross-bridge bus services were in operation within an hour or so of the bridge being declared open by the Governor of Macau. That day the whole of the territory was enjoying something of a carnival atmosphere and by the evening every available bus was being pressed into service, regardless of the timetable, to cater for the happy crowds who wanted to sample an 'over the sea' bus ride. Gross overloading was unavoidable and uncontrollable as the single-decker buses were enthusiastically besieged! CTPEMI's shortage of reserve rolling-stock inevitably meant that it had to be "Fok Lei's" vehicles which dominated the scene on that hectic Sunday evening of 5th October 1974 and for the remainder of that busy weekend.

4—Other Bus and Coach Operations

Since at least the early 1970's—and probably before—the Kee Kwan Motor Road Company has operated cross-border services; local at first but by 1980 a service to Canton (Guangzhou) was introduced. This service quickly became popular with local people of Chinese origin but, as China slowly relaxed, this has become a major tourist route using modern vehicles.

In the 1970's, the only coaches to be seen in Macau were a handful for use as school or factory workers buses, a few to take tourists on very limited sightssing tours and staff buses for the casinos. Amongst the tourist coaches, British chassis prevailed, ioncluding a few Seddon rear-engined models as well as the usual Ford/Bedford/Commer/ BMC range

By 1981, as China slowly opened its doors to foreigners, the development of Macau–China tourism brought about the introduction of more comfortable coaching and, to cater for 'package tour' groups, a small number of 'tourist-

coaches' of exclusively Japanese origin operated from a parking place adjacent to the Lisboa Hotel—itself a remarkable piece of architecture. One particular type of Isuzu was almost identical to the Kee Kwan local service buses, having the same high, gaunt looking body-style and may have been part of the latter's operation as the Chinese authorities appeared at that time to prefer only one cross-border operation per crossing point.

By 1984, while the products of Nissan and Mitsubishi were in evidence, there were quite a number of British Ford models—possibly including chassis assembled at a short-lived plant within Guangdong Province, adjoining Hong Kong.

Since that time the major Japanese manufacturers have provided the majority of Macau's coach requirements and, with the development of long-distance coaching, many of these are modern air-conditioned vehicles built to international standards of comfort.

5—Restructuring of Bus Operations in 1988

While it is the primary function of this book to describe the 'British Bus Years', it is felt appropriate to include a brief description of events between the demise of the traditional British buses and the arrival of the first Dennis Darts late in 1995. It should be pointed-out that the fleet of Albions were, indeed, extant for much of that period and the last double-deckers ran in the late 1980's.

The late 1980's saw major change when a complete reformation of bus services took place. The two operators of local services, described in detail in earlier chapters, "Fok Lei" and CTPEMI, had, since the opening of the first bridge to Taipa—in 1974—kept largely to their own traditional operating areas, according to the terms of their 1974 franchises. The only "Fok Lei" intrusion onto the two islands was on cross-bridge routes operated jointly with CTPEMI—and vice versa. No routes were operated by "Fok Lei" wholly within the islands and, likewise, no route was operated wholly within Macau City by CTPEMI.

All this was to change and, following restructuring, both "Fok Lei" and CTPEMI re-emerged with new trading names and with a shared operating area covering the whole territory. The 'new' companies adopted new titles,with shortened trading names used in the public domain. The former "Fok Lei" became Transportes Ubarnos de Macau—or 'Transmac' while CTPEMI became Sociedade de Transportes Collectivos de Macau, S.A.R.L.— 'TCM'.

Both operators introduced a fleet numbering system, with, at first, all vehicles clearly marked. In some cases, however, fleet numbers have not been maintained.

Bus Routes in 1974-75

"Fok Lei"

1   Barra to Porta Ilha Verde
2   Circular: Estacao Central to Canidrome
3   Estacao Central to Pont Cais (hydrofoil & ferry piers)
4   Carreira "Peouema Vo Tadela" to Cipade
5   Barra to Porta do Cerco

Estacao Central : Central Bus Station

Additional routes from 1975

5A   Barra to Hospital (visiting hours only)
11   Estacao Central to Ilha de Taipa island and village
21   Estacao Central to Coloane island and village) via Taipa
21A Estacao Central to Hac Sa (Coloane island)via Taipa

Taipa Island 1974
Ferry Pier to Taipa Village

Coloane Island 1974
Coloane Village Ferry pier to a point a little beyond Ka Ho Village

Causeway route
Taipa Village to Coloane Village/Ferry Pier

CTPEMI *from early 1975—as above (no route numbers) plus Routes 11, 21 & 21A—joint operation with "Fok Lei" except that Macau terminus was two hundred metres past the bus station (not shared with "Fok Lei").*

Bus Routes in 1995

TRANSMAC Bus Routes

1   Fai Chi Kei - Barra
2   P.Serenidade - A.V. Morais , ALM Robeiro - CEM,Areia-Oreta - P.Serenidade
3   NovoTerminal - Portas Do Cerco
3A   NovoTerminal - Portas E Horta
4   Fai Chi Kei - Lin Fung Miu. R. Campo. Alm. Lacerda - Fai Chi Kei
5   Barra - Almieda, Horta E Costa, Lin Fung Miu. Jai Alai - Barra
6   P. Serenidade - AV. Morais, Barra, Lisboa. Rodrigues. Alm. Ribeiro, Horta E Costa, Iao Hon - P. Serenidade
7   Rua I De Bairro Iao Hon - ALM. Ribeiro. R. Campo, Fai Chi Kei - Rua I De Bairro Iao Hon
8   Ilha Verde - Carlos Da Maia, Barra, Areia Preta - Ilha Verde
8A   Ilha Verde - Horta E Costa, Cabral, R. Campo, Kiang Wu, Areia Preta - Ilha Verde
9   Portas Do Cerco - Barra - P. Do Cerco
9A   Portas Do Cerco - H. Estoril, Lisboa, Barbosa,- P. Do Cerco
11   Ponte E Horta - Hyatt - Vila Taipa, Jockey Club - Ponle E Hona
16B Barbosa (Canal Das Hortas) - B. Barbosa (Canal Das Hortas)
26   Fai Chi Kei · Hyatt, Taipa - Vila Coloane - Fai Chi Kei
26A Fai Chi Kei - Hac Sa
28A Nova Terminal - Vila Taipa, Nova Terminal.

28B Ilha Verde - Lisboa - Ilha Verde
28B (Partial) Ilha Verde - H. Lisboa
28C Jai Alai - P. do Cerco - Jai Alai
32   Fai Chi Kei - Tunel. Lisboa, Jai Alai - Fai Chi Kei
33   Fai Chi Kei - Vila Tapia - Fai Chi Kei
38   Esc. Comercial - Jockey Club
AP1 Aeroporto - Jetfoil - Hotels - City - Portas do Cerco

TCM Bus Routes

10   Barra - Cerco
10A Barra - Jetfoil
11   Barra - V. Taipa
12   Iao Hon - Jelfoil
14   Taipa - Hac Sa
15   Coloane - Ka Ho
17   Camoes - Camoes
19   Iao Hon - R. CamDo, Alm. Ribeiro, Camoes - Iao Hon
21   Barra - V. Coloane
21A Barra - Hac Sa
22   Iao Hon - Jockey Club
22   (Desdobramento) Iao Hon - U.M.
23   Cerco - Cor. Mesquila, H. Lisboa, Jetfoil Horta E Costa, Areil Prea - Cerco
25   Cerco - Fai Chi Kei. . H. Lisboa - U.M. V. Coloane -Cerco
AP1 Aeroporto - Jetfoil - Hotels - City - Portas do Cerco

Chapter Two
The Buses of "Fok Lei"

Ford (Canada)

Approximately 15 Canadian Ford buses, based on World War Two military lorry chassis, were inherited from the former Public Bus Company when "Fok Lei" acquired their services and vehicles-probably in 1952. Registration numbers, in the old Macau series, included M4*/6/9/23/46/47*/54*/96/563*—*indicates numbers which have been confirmed from photographs; remainder unconfirmed, but were M100 plus.

Photographic evidence suggests that Perkins diesel engines were fitted in at least some of these Fords although they would have almost certainly been petrol engined when new. The semi-forward-control chassis was fitted with single rear tyres and was relatively high from the ground as would be expected from a military vehicle.

The bodywork bore more than a passing resemblance to that fitted to Hong Kong lorry-buses of the period and it is not beyond the realms of possibility that they had once been the property of either Kowloon Motor Bus or China Motor Bus. Despite their small size, two entrances were provided

LEFT: M.563 running on Route 4 in 1953 does not show a Perkins badge and may have still been petrol engined.

TOP RIGHT: This rear view of one of the Fords reveals that it had a rounded rear dome and a route number display

LOWER LEFT: M.47, on Route 5, clearly displays its Perkins Diesel badge on the radiator. The front, or scuttle, was typical of contemporary military vehicles

CENTRE RIGHT: This side view of one of the Canadian Ford buses on a military lorry chassis clearly shows the "Fok Lei" company name in Portuguese and Chinese along the side panels. *(All from the F. W. York collection*

From J. Shearman's 1974 notebook:

These fleet lists are based on personal observations as at early July 1973, mid-January 1974 and mid-June 1974. Any changes in the situation at these times are noted; otherwise no change.

It is virtually certain that the following lists include every bus existing at the above times which is, or has been, used on public bus services in the Province.

The lists should be read with close reference to the text which provides full details and descriptions of the vehicles.

Although registration numbers give some indication of the order of vehicle acquisition, there are some instances of reissuing numbers as is obvious from certain private cars. Furthermore, some buses, or perhaps groups of buses appear to exchange registrations amongst themselves whilst they are undergoing major body rebuilding. In consequence, the only meaningful way to identify buses in Macau is by individual vehicle description and not by registration numbers. Thus these fleet lists state that there is, for example, a Bristol L5G with a certain type of body, which, at a particular date, is carrying registration number such and such and not that such and such registration number always identifies a particular bus. This should be firmly born in mind when reading these fleet lists as this is not the customary method used for a fleet list of a British operator.

The above list shows the situations as at July 1973, mid-January 1974 and mid-June 1974 except that:

i) at 1/74 M-10-70 & M-27-75 had exchanged reg nos

ii) " " M-11-03 & M-19-07 had exchanged reg nos

iii) at 6/74 M-14-02 & M-14-10 had exchanged reg. nos

iv) in May a fire in the depot totally destroyed the body of M-12-47 and damaged the offside of M-27-06.

Liberty (China)

The Chinese-built Liberty Bus was a left-hand-drive vehicle built in Shanghai. "Fok Lei" at one time owned one example but it is reported to have sold it back to China. No dates have become available as to when the vehicle was in "Fok Lei" ownership.

Thornycroft

Two Thornycroft CD4LW Cygnets were purchased second-hand from the China Motor Bus Co., of Hong Kong Island, probably in 1958, when CMB withdrew many pre-war Cygnets. These buses were powered by Gardner 4LW engines and had CMB designed teak-framed bodywork.

Vulcan

One Vulcan half-cab single-deck bus was also purchased second-hand from CMB, again probably in 1958. Bodywork was the same as the Thornycroft's but the engine was the larger 85bhp Gardner 5LW.

PHOTOGRAPHS

No photographs have become available to illustrate the Liberty, Thornycroft or Vulcan types. Should any person have anything, however indistinct, please write to the publishers who would like you to contact them.

Bristol L5G-type single-deckers

The Bristol L-type was introduced in 1937 to replace the single-deck version of the G-series and remained in production until 1941 when wartime conditions prevailed. The L was reintroduced in 1946 and continued until 1950 -except for additional chassis built for specific requirements in 1954. Macau had examples spanning the period 1939 to 1950.

The oldest Bristol L5G 's in Macau were a pair dating from 1939, which came from the West Yorkshire Road Car Co. Ltd., together with another similar pair of 1941 vintage Old photographs show two such buses, with their original Macau registrations of M.86 and M.87, complete with West Yorkshire-style painted wooden destination boards, externally illuminated. The actual destination appeared in large Chinese characters, with a smaller Portuguese version above.

From such records as have become available, it is possible that two of the four, later known by the fleet

Vehicle Specifications: Bristol L5G	
Chassis:	Bristol L5G*
Engine:	Gardner 5LW*, 7-litre, nominally 95 bhp.
Gearbox:	Bristol 5-speed (some possibly 4-speed)manual, some later replaced by new David Brown units
Brakes:	Vacuum-servo (triple-servo system)
Body & layout:	1974–as 'original' ½-cabs: B33+12FEX, REX,G,sc as rebuilt/rebodied–various - see following text.
Date built:	1939-1950
Dates rebodied:	i) as ½-cabs - 1975-80 ii) as full-front - 1982-84
Introduced to Macau:	1956-64
Length:	27ft 6in
Width:	7ft 6in
Height:	Approx 10ft (standard ECW body)
Wheelbase:	17ft 6in

NOTE: * indicates that there were exceptions before export to Macau. Please refer to the text for clarification.

numbers L101/2, 113/4, were the original M.86 and M.87. The first Bristol L5G's entered service in Macau in late 1956 or early 1957. As already mentioned, registration numbers were routinely changed at overhaul, there only having been 28 registration numbers issued to cover 30 vehicles (including the breakdown crane), making the usual methods of keeping track of vehicles by kerbside observation impossible, especially as registrations were also changed from two to four numbers some years after the early Bristol arrived in Macau. In order to rationalize the situation, fleet numbers were introduced in 1974 as a permanent identity but, as it was impossible to ascertain actual dates of acquisition, "Fok Lei" numbered their Bristol L5G's in chassis number sequence. Within five years, however, the fleet numbers had been discontinued.

IMPORTANT NOTE:
It is stressed that the means used to identify the above thirty vehicles was by physically checking their chassis number plates—or the numbers stamped into the steel frames—in 1974, in Macau. It was by working back from those that the UK registration numbers have been derived. The identities were **not** determined from UK registration numbers or from any UK records which were unavailable in Macau at the time.

LEFT OPPOSITE: M.86—ex West Yorkshire Road Car Co—was one of the first Bristol L5G buses to enter service in Macau and in this view had not been modified for the hot humid climate as it retains the three half-drop opening windows each side. As these are closed, this was probably a winter photograph. Also retained at this stage was the bodyside moulding and hand painted, externally illuminated, destination board. *(Ho Kun Meng*

RIGHT: Another of the first batch of Bristol L5G's with "Fok Lei" seen here passing Largo do Senado some time later, having gained a full set of tropical-style sliding windows but still with the painted destination board. *(Mike Davis collection*

BRISTOL L5G   Fleet list as fleet numbered 1974—L101-L130

Chassis number	Year chassis built	UK regn number	Col. 4	Body at export: make	number	layout	Date to UK dealer or* exported	Macau fleet number	July 1974 Macau reg. no.	Notes
48.029	1939	CWY 981	WY	ECW	6226/1	B32F	1956	L101	M-10-46	
48.030	1939	CWY 982	WY	ECW	6227/1	B32F	1956	L102	M-10-71	
48.053	1939	CVF 847	ECL	ECW	6253/1	B35R	1957	L103	M-10-72	
48.05(?)[1]	1939	CVF 846[1]	ECL	ECW	6252/1	B35R	1957[1]	L104X	M-12-09	[1] Details presume that bus was 48.052 —see text.
48.095	1939	DDV 33	SN	Beadle	?	B36R	1959	L105	M-19-07	
48.100	1939	DDV 38	SN	Beadle	?	B36R	1959	L106	M-10-70	
48.125	1939	CVF 856	ECL	ECW	6259/1	B35R	1957	L107	M-10-50	
50.024	1939	CVF 876	ECL	ECW	6281/1	DP32R	1957	L108	M-10-74	
(50.073?)[2]	1941	(HAE 12?)	BT	BBW u	?	DP31R	1960/1	L109	M-14-02	[2] Low PV2 radiator fitted 2/56 Details presume that bus was 50.073
50.088[3]	1941	DFH 451 [4]	BT	ECW u	3329/2	B35R	1962[4]	L110	M-16-04	[3] Low PV2 radiator fitted 3/56 - [4] see Note 4 below
52.021	1940	DOD 510	WN	Beadle	?	B36R	1962	L111	M-10-86	
52.084	1940	DOD 527	SN	Beadle	?	B36R	1962	L112	M-14-10	
52.051	1941	DWW 589	WY	ECW	6734/1	B32F	1956	L113	deregistered	
52.056	1941	DWW 594	WY	ECW	6739/1	B32F	1956	L114	deregistered	
61.106	1947	EWY 422	WY	ECW	1276/2	B35R	1964	L115	M-27-05	
63.005	1947	FPW 514	ECO	ECW	1317/2	B35R	1963	L116	M-29-83	
63.068	1947	FPW 519	ECO	ECW	1360/2	B35R	1964*	L117	M-27-74	
63.132	1947	JHT 848	BT	ECW	1422/2	B33D	1960*	L118	M-11-76	
63.114	1947	JHT 852	BT	ECW	1418/2	B33D	1960*	L119	M-11-02	
63.170	1947	JHT 863	BT	ECW	1433/2	B33D	1960*	L120	M-11-19	
63.197	1947	FPW 526	ECO	ECW	1407/2	B35R	1964*	L121	M-27-51	
67.099	1948	LHT 905	BT	BBW u	?	B35R	1964*	L122	M-10-87	
71.126	1949	LHN 805	UAS	ECW	4113/2	B35R	1965*	L123	M-27-06	
71.176	1949	LHN 814	UAS	ECW	4121/2	B35R	1965*	L124	M-14-77	
73.143R	1949	LHN 566	UAS	ECW	3365/2	B35R	1965*	L125	M-27-75	
73.163R	1949	LHN 586	UAS	ECW	3385/2	B35R	1965*	L126	M-19-01	
79.037	1950	LHN 849	UAS	ECW	4156/2	B35R	1965*	L127	M-28-61	
79.042	1950	LHN 856	UAS	ECW	(4163/2?)	B35R	1965*	L128	M-12-47	
79.107	1950	MHW 995	UAS	ECW	3999/2	B35R	1966*	L129	M-11-03	
79.127	1950	MHW 998	UAS	ECW	4003/2	B35R	1966*	L130	M-14-18	

NOTE: Where bracketed numbers include a question mark, eg (50.073?) this indicates an uncertainty.

Key to Column 4: WY: West Yorkshire Road Car Company   SN: Southern National Omnibus Company
ECO: Eastern Counties Omnibus Company   BT: Bristol Tramways & Carriage Company
ECL: Eastern Counties Omnibus Company,   WN: Western National Omnibus Company
     via Lincolnshire Road Car Co.   UAS: United Automobile Services

Note u: Indicates a used (second-hand) body fitted by UK operator in 1956 (50.073 & 50.088) or 1957 (67.099).

Note 4: Chassis 50.088 was definately with "Fok Lei". This renders the record of this vehicle being with Rogers of Redcar suspect. The 'DFH 451' noted with Rogers was probably not 50.088 but another vehicle which lost its true registration number identity. This strongly suggests a case of unofficial registration number swapping in the UK. It is unlikely that an export order placed by "Fok Lei" would have been met from an independent operator rather than from the BTC operators.

All the Bristol L5G's were fitted with Gardner 5LW engines which, in all but three cases, were the engines installed as new in England. The three exceptions, one AEC and two Bristol units, were replaced at some time prior to being exported to Macau, so that all should be regarded as L5G models. One bus, L128, had a reconditioned 5LW engine purchased from China Motor Bus Co. in 1974. This unit gave the best performance of any in the fleet, having been fitted in a 25ft long Guy Arab Mk IV and had been set for use on hilly Hong Kong routes.

The transmission of the Bristol L5G's was, in all cases, through a dry plate clutch and manual 'crash' gearbox which could be either four or five speed. Earlier examples had the standard Bristol pre-war wartime radiator, high mounted and with straight sides, while post-war versions, (and two 1941 conversions) had the lower mounted and more rounded PV2 type.

Most of Macau's Bristol L5G's had original bodywork built by Eastern Coachworks (ECW) but there were exceptions—Beadle and Bristol Body Works (BBW). Most examples were so extensively rebuilt that they resembled the original only in outline. Flaired skirt-panels and some beading disappeared; dual entrances—forward and rear—became standard and were protected by the Macau-style swing gate, sprung to close when released. All bodies at this stage were of this layout, with 33 seats plus a nominal 12 standees.

Many of the L5G's had, in 1974, retained their original cast aluminium clutch cover plate on which was cast the initials of the body builder, ie ECW or Beadle— a few, however, were blank and probably stem from chassis rebodied by BBW.

Until 1975, Fok Lei" had rebuilt and rebodied buses using the original ECW framework, which was originally of hardwood. The use of aluminium alloy by ECW commenced in March 1948 with body number 2410. ECW bodied L5G's which went to Macau with body

number 3365 and above were constructed principally of aluminium.

Descriptions of the Bristol L5G's are set out on the following pages in two groups—buses of pre- and post-war build. Within these groups, vehicles from the same operator are described collectively, even when not delivered at the same time.

Where a vehicle was later altered substantially or re-bodied it will be illustrated separately in a sub-section devoted to the development of the type after the core period—1973 to 1975—being discussed here in the main vehicle description. Included in this group are those few Bristols which were, from 1975, rebodied by coachworks in Hong Kong to a modern design, in all cases retaining the original exposed Bristol radiator. Others were rebodied by "Fok Lei", in their own workshops

Every one of the 30 Bristol L5G's survived in daily use in 1978, although one had long since become a crane truck. A long serving employee of "Fok Lei" told one author, in 1974, that there was once a shortened L5G which was tried-out on routes in narrow streets with tight corners. It is not clear whether this was a shortened overhang or a shortened wheelbase, but adds weight to the story that the breakdown crane did, possibly, operate for a short time as a short wheelbase bus

Pre-war Bristol L5G chassis

L101, L102, L113 and L114

Ex West Yorkshire Road Car Co Ltd

These buses were purchased via UK dealer Colbro— but through a Hong Kong agent—probably in 1956, having been new to West Yorkshire Road Car Co in 1939 and 1940. The chassis were to standard 'prewar' Bristol L5G specification which remained unaltered in Macau days. Chassis numbers of the 1939 vintage pair were 48.029 & 48.030 and were originally registered CWY 981 & CWY 982 in Yorkshire, becoming "Fok Lei" L101 and L102 when that fleet was numbered in 1974. The 1941 buses had chassis numbers 52.051 and 52.056 and had

similarly been DWW 589 and DWW 594, becoming L113 & L114 in Macau.

Upon arrival in Macau, the original ECW bodies remained largely unaltered for some years, with stylishly flared skirt panels, waist-rail mouldings and even retaining and utilising the distinctive West Yorkshire exter-

RIGHT: The bus that had been either West Yorkshire DWW 589 or DWW 594—and was later to become L113 or L114—standing engineless and damaged in the street outside the 'old' depot yard near Barra terminus in 1973. The original flaired skirt panels and moulded waist rail clearly in evdence. *(John Shearman*

subsequent addition of a second doorway behind the rear wheelarch. Both the new and original entrances were provided with the style of inwardly opening swing gate particular to "Fok Lei".

Ironically, it was the two newer bodies—formerly DWW 589 and nally illuminated destination indicator which took the form of a painted board showing sign-written information—sometimes referred to as 'Bible' indicators. Destination boxes and roller blinds were subsequently fitted to all four.

DWW 594—which were scrapped first, probably because they had been rebuilt least and they retained their flared skirt panels and stylish mouldings until physically broken-up in 1974 by which time both had been lying derelict for some time, one having been in use as a shed and the other was engineless and abandoned. They both retained to the end the three-rear-window arrangement, although the original emergency door had been replaced by plain panelling—probably after the provision of a second, rear, service doorway. Their chassis were rebodied in 1975 (*qv*) to take their rightful place as L113 and 114.

A photograph on page 16 shows one of these buses, then registered M.86, in service in Macau but retaining the three half-drop windows each side—possibly they entered service in the cool winter months. Another photograph shows M.87 with a complete set of windows with full-depth sliding glass to provide better ventilation in the hot and humid climate.

It is believed that the two original Macau Bristol L5G's—initially registered M.86 and M.87—were one or other pair of this quartet.

When built in 1939/40, these bodies, to West Yorkshire specification, with so-called 'porch' style front entrances, required a rear emergency exit and this was placed in the rear panel. Two small windows, curved at the top, were located, one either side of the central door—which itself had a window—giving a three window rear aspect.

L101 and L102 from 1973

The bodies of the two buses that became L101 and L102—chassis 48.029 & 48.030—had, by 1973, been rebuilt to a very great extent but without losing the essential qualities that identify an ECW product. The prewar ECW body was based on a timber frame which was largely and progressively replaced by "Fok Lei" coachbuilders who omitted the distinctive flared skirt.

At this distance in time, it is impossible to say if one or more entered service with the single front doorway but what can be certain is that this arrangement would have quickly proved to be very inconvenient and led to the

ABOVE: L102 at Barra terminus, shows the offside of the heavily rebuilt—possibly rebodied—pre-war style of ECW body. Although taken in May 1975, the full-depth sliding windows are firmly shut to keep out the heavy rain that day. *(Mike Davis*

The completed rebuild was a very businesslike, but plain, reproduction of the original design, very basically appointed, with no frills. The three rear windows of these two bodies were replaced by a single, standard, 'post-war' ECW-style, rectangular glass. Despite these changes, the character of the original bodywork was still discernable, even without the flared skirts, mouldings and beading. Side windows all had full-depth sliding panes in every bay. As rebuilt, the seating/layout remained B33+12FEXG,REXG.

The demise of these two buses came sometime between 1978 and 1982 but it is possible that the vehicle that became the second breakdown tender in the early 1980's was one of the pair but this cannot be said for certain.

L113 & L114—rebodying

As noted above, by 1974 these two buses were out of service—because their bodies were life-expired, even by Macau standards—but were being retained for later rebodying.

Early in 1975, the bodies were stripped from the chassis and the latter refurbished to a very high standard before being shipped to Hong Kong where they were to be rebodied—L113 by Metro-Dodwell Motors and L114 by Union Auto Body Builders (*qv*).

L103, L104X, L107 & L108
ex-Lincolnshire Road Car Co
—new to Eastern Counties Omnibus Co

These four buses were sold by Lincolnshire in 1957, having been new to Eastern Counties as CVF 847, CVF(846?), CVF856 and CVF 876 with Chassis numbers 48.053, 48.05(2?), 48.125 and 50.024. The bracketed figures are the subject of some debate as, when the chassis plates of all the Macau L5G's were examined in 1974, that of L104X was damaged and the last digit, now thought to be 2, was difficult to read but if correct, so is CVF 846.

It is believed that these four buses arrived at "Fok Lei", via Hong Kong agents, in two pairs—that being the company's purchasing policy—probably in 1957 and/or 1958.

The ECW bodywork was generally to the same standard pre-war profile as L101 etc, but, in this case, all four had rear-entrances, originally with sliding doorways and offside emergency doorways in the first bay behind the driver.

In the absence of an emergency door in the rear of the body, there were only two rear windows, again having distinctively curved upper margins which, together, could be loosely described as being like a 'D' rotated through 90 degrees. They

LEFT: Sister bus, L101, leaves Barra on the same day with its front swing gate open and the rear one closed. By this time it was usual for the lower part of the radiator surround to have been replaced, emphasising the high-style of the pre-war model. *(Mike Davis*

ABOVE: Registration number M-10-72 was being carried by the former Eastern Counties bus CVF 847 which had recently been fleet numbered L103 by "Fok Lei", although the fleet number was not carried. Bodywork on this bus was similar to L101 etc ecxept that rear entrances were fitted from new. Seen here in March 1975 on Route 5. *(Mike Davis*

were divided by a pillar which was narrower at the bottom than at the top.

The buses that became L103/4/7 were 35-seaters in England with L108 having been a 32-seater.

Modifications for service in Macau were generally of a similar nature to those carried out on L101 etc., with the exception that the additional doorway—strictly speaking a gateway—was added at the front, in the first body bay, immediately behind the front wheel. The original sliding doors were removed by "Fok Lei" and gates fitted to both entrances in their dual-doorway guise.

L103 & L108

After the bodies of L103 and 108 had been rebuilt, they were virtually indistinguishable from L101 & 102, having the simplified 'ECW' outline produced by "Fok Lei" craftsmen.

L108, however, differed in at least two respects; firstly in having a flat-fronted canopy over the cab, somewhat reminiscent of the China Motor Bus (Hong Kong) Guy Arab MkIV's with 'Birmingham' fronts, and, secondly, in having its rear doorway fitted with a manually operated, two-leaf, folding door in place of the more

RIGHT: M-10-72— This offside view of what is believed to have become L103 was taken in January 1973, over two years before the top picture. The high-mounted radiator had been repaired with a new bottom section by "Fok Lei". *(E. L. Rees*

ABOVE: Only the third yellow single-deck L5G in the "Fok Lei" fleet, L108 was rebuilt somewhat differently to its contemporaries in having a flat front to the canopy and flush mounted destination screen. Another difference was the fitting of a manually-operated folding door inside the rear entrance. As this was usually left open and out of use, it is hard to detect in this March 1975 photograph. *(Mike Davis)*

usual gate. It was only the third single-deck bus to receive the 1974/5 yellow livery.

It is possible to argue that the rear steps, or rather their side framing, retained the profile of the original flaired skirts until the buses were withdrawn. Critical comparison with the shape of the equivalent fitting at the front could show this to be the case.

L107

L107 was not so drastically rebuilt as L103 and 108 and remained in more original form until, in 1975, its body was scrapped and the reconditioned chassis sent to Hong Kong for rebodying by Union Auto (*qv*).

L104X

By the time that the fleet was numbered in 1974, the fourth chassis in this group had been shortened—the wheel-base being reduced to about 12ft and the rear overhang removed—and converted to a breakdown tender similar in style to many used by contemporary BTC operators in the UK, hence its having an L-series number but with an X suffix. This served both to place it in its correct position in the table of Bristol L5G's and to indicate that it was something other than a bus. Unfortunately, as related below, the chassis number is now considered to have been another and is thus out of numerical order.

L104X was created from the Bristol L5G chassis thought

LEFT: L104X was a shortened L5G chassis with no rear overhang. Contrarary to previously published data, the chassis number of the 1974 "Fok Lei" breakdown crane, then numbered L104X points to it having been CVF 846 in the Eastern Counties fleet. *(Mike Davis*

LEFT: The problems of identifying buses by registration number are highlighted by this January 1973 photograph of an L5G with distinctive Beadle cab windscreen, taken more than 18-months before the fleet was carefully chronicled from July 1974, at which time this number, M-14-02, was being carried by chassis number 50.073, fitted with a BBW body. In the period from June 1974 onwards, no Beadle bodied bus ever carried this number. (E. L. Rees

to have been 48.052. The last figure on the chassis number plate was damaged but was at first considered to have been '6'. The preceeding figures were, however, without any doubt 48.05... Further research has established that 48.056 was *most unlikely* and after very careful consideration, chassis number 48.052 is now believed to be more likely. Unfortunately the incorrect number has previously been published.

Assuming that the chassis number in question was as suspected, then the chassis was one which once carried ECW body No6252/1, similar to that on L103 (B35R),with a rear doorway, and was operated by Eastern Counties, registered CVF 846.

The author was once assured that this vehicle did originally operate in Macau as a full-length bus. It might be that 104 was the vehicle which became the short bus referred to earlier prior to its finally being converted to a breakdown crane.

L105, L106, L111 & L112

New to Southern National Omnibus Co

These four high-radiator Bristol L5G's were initially registered in England in 1940 as DDV 33, DDV 38, DOD 510 and DOD 527 respectively—chassis numbers 48.095, 48.100, 52.021 and 52.034—bodied when new by Mumfords of Plymouth. Strictly speaking, DOD 510 was, operated by Western National but the Western and SOuthern National fleets were fleets were well integrated.

Southern National had them all rebodied by Beadle in 1950 to an approximation of the then current ECW design— with the exception of the windscreen and front bulkhead windows which were to Beadle's then standard drsign, with a markedly curved lower margin, often referred to as 'drooping'.

As new—and upon arrival in Macau—all these buses had rear doorways which were fitted with sliding doors, being B35R. As with all other buses arriving so equipped, "Fok Lei" introduced an additional entrance at the front to ease boarding and alighting, giving the standard revised

layout of B33+12FEXG,REXG.

Rebuilding work over the years resulted, by 1973/74, in bodies which resembled the prewar ECW design as similarly rebuilt by "Fok Lei" but still with the distinguishing windscreen and, on L105 & 106, front bulkhead window*frames*—the actual glazing having been replaced by rectangular sliding glass. The charactistic flat, narrow, panel above the side windows, separated from the roof by a beading strip, had disappeared, probably after replacement roof-hoops had been fitted. An exception to this was the bus which became L106 (formerly DDV 38) which was photographed as late as 1976, still with the post-war style of roof profile. Rectangular rear windows from the Beadle design were retained.

L105

The body of L105 was given a very heavy rebuild in 1975 which resulted in it losing its last remaining Beadle features, the windscreen and front window frames. The body was also altered to have a front and centre entrance in association with the introduction of a seated conductress (sc).

Certain features—notably, the shape of the destination box with a pronounced radius to the top corners and the position of the marker lights, either side of the destination screen—help to identify this rebuilt body as that which had borne registration number M-19-07 (L105). It is thus, on this rare occasion, safe to assume that a prolonged period in workshops passed without the usual number-swapping as the completed bus was returned to the road once again as M-19-07.

An additional small side destination screen was provided at the top of the side window located between the two doorways as was the seat for the seated conductress. The revised body layout was B29FEG,CXG(sc). The top of the driver's windscreen was inset by about 5cm (2ins) into the canopy, following the Beadle line which had previously been concealed by the rain shield. At this time, swing gates were retained. L105 was the first bus painted by "Fok Lei" to have fleet numbers applied. A coat of yellow paint completed this transformation.

TOP LEFT: M-19-07 was, or may have been—due to registration number swapping—the bus that later became L105. It was photographed here in 1973 having been rebuilt—possibly even rebodied—with only the curve of the windscreen as a reminder that this was once a Beadle body. *(E. L. Rees*

CENTRE LEFT: L105 as it returned to service in May 1975 in yellow livery and complete with fleet number on the front dash panel. It is believed that this really was chassis 48.095. The swing gates remain in use but provision for the later introduction of a seated conductress was made by having a centre exit. *(John Shearman collection*

LOWER LEFT: The bus that became L106—formerly DDV 38—was fitted with a second-hand Beadle body in 1950 by Southern National, its previous operator, and it still retained some of its distinctive features in this 1976 view . It was the first—and possibly only—red L5G to carry its fleet number. It was seen here in 1976 in very colonial surroundings. *(Derek Lucas*

L109 & L110

ex Bristol Omnibus Co. Ltd.

Like many wartime Bristols that were rebodied after the war, these two buses had acquired low mounted post-war PV2 radiators when the chassis were rebodied while with Bristol Omnibus.

From the chassis numbers it would appear that these two were what became known as 'unfrozen' chassis, although the chassis numbers—50.073 (unconfirmed) and 50.088—were in the same series as buses produced in 1939. After deciding to restrict, or 'freeze', all bus production in 1941, the Government subsequently permitted manufacturers to complete those chassis on which work had commenced. Thus these two Bristols were not delivered until 1941, having been 'unfrozen'.

L109: there is a small degree of doubt over the chassis number and for the purposes of this description, it is assumed to be 50.073. That being so, then the British registration number was HAE 12.

L110 had previously been DFH 45 having originally been allocated to Gloucester City Services, a subsidiary of Bristol Tramways.

The original, 1941, bodies were BBW but, in 1956, these were replaced by further second-hand bodies but this time of post-war pattern.

HAE 12 (No 2162) was rebodied using the 1950 BBW-built body originally on the chassis of Bristol No 2204. It was withdrawn by Bristol in October 1960 when it was sold to AMCC, a London dealer with associations with the export of buses to Macau.

Chassis 50.088 was *definitely* with "Fok Lei". This renders the record elsewhere of this vehicle being with Rogers of Redcar suspect. The 'DFH 451' noted with Rogers was probably not 50.088 but another vehicle which lost its true registration number identity. This strongly suggests a case of unofficial registration number swapping in the UK. It is highly unlikely that an export order placed by "Fok Lei" would have been met from an independent operator rather than from the BTC operators. Chassis 50.088 received the 1949 ECW-built body (no 3329) from bus No 2197. It was sold by Bristol in October 1962 but reports that it saw further UK service with Rogers of Redcar before they sold it in December 1964 must, surely, be suspect.

The bodies of both L109 & 110 were to the standard Tilling Group post-war outline designed by ECW with a flatter roof and flat side panels—or cant panels— between the top of the side windows and the commencement of the curve of the roof, from which it was divided by a beading strip. This design was without the pre-war refinements of flared skirt panels, neat moulding and beading. The sides of these more recent bodies were somewhat higher in profile than the older type.

During 1975 and 1976, L109 and L110 were rebodied again, this time by "Fok Lei", which utilised the original body framework.

L109 resembled the original style, except that the original rear entrance was moved to the centre. There was also a front entrance, making it possible to operate these buses with a seated conductress, when the layout was altered to B29FEG,CXG(sc).

ABOVE: This July 1974 rear view of what is believed to have been chassis 50.073 with BBW bodywork shows the rear destination box—complete with broken glass. This bus was awaiting a major body rebuild, from which it emerged as M-11-19—as shown below. *(John Shearman*

ABOVE: M-16-04 seen here in January 1973, still showing clearly the distinctive BBW beading as applied to its 'express' or 'dual-purpose' bodies. Another distinctive BBW feature is the provision of square-cornered side-window vents. It is thought that, with registration number swapping rife in Macau, this bus probably exchanged registrations with its sister ex-Bristol vehicle with ECW body and later became L109. The body seen here was acquired by this chassis in 1956 at which time the lower post-war PV2 radiator was fitted. *(E. L. Rees*

LEFT: L109 was rebuilt by "Fok Lei" using the original body—probably BBW—frame and as such retained much of its traditional appearance. It was photographed in April 1975, soon after returning to traffic as a front/centre 'gateway' bus and in the then new yellow and cream livery. *(Mike Davis*

Post-war Bristol L5G's

From the recommencement of single-deck bus body production, ECW introduced a new design which was not merely a pre-war concept revamped. The roof was far flatter than before as a result of the flat side panels above the side windows being extended upwards by about 300mm (12 inches)and separated from the actual roof by a beading strip which curved downwards at the extreme front and rear. It is suggested that this was intended to allow advertising that could not otherwise be carried in a suitably asthetic manner on a single-deck bus.

The stylish flared skirt panels were not a feature of post-ECW body styling, nor were moulded waistrail panels, although 'express' bodies—sometimes known as 'dual-purpose vehicles'—with high backed seats in a bus body shell, were treated to an application of trim in the form of two rows of beading strip, narrowed towards the rear, and often painted between in a contrasting colour to that of the main livery. Macau had one example of these.

ABOVE: This photograph of M-27-05 was taken in 1966 and it is believed that the registration number remained with this bus until it became L115 in 1974. (H.Piercy

Until 1949, the body framing was of timber construction but aluminium alloy was gradually introduced during that year and all buses thereafter—as opposed to coaches—were thus constructed.

L115—The earliest Post-War L5G ex-West Yorkshire Road Car Co Ltd

This was the oldest post-war Bristol L model in the "Fok Lei" fleet, being chassis number 61.106 of 1947 (EWY 422). L115, like all post-war L5G's was fitted with the post-war PV2 radiator.

Its ECW body, which was rebuilt by West Yorkshire in 1956, was B35R, but in Macau it became B33FEXG,REXG and was distinguishable from earlier bodies, as shown above, by the higher profile. It was withdrawn by West Yorkshire in 1964 and there are reports that it was exported by Norths, the dealer, in 1965 but, although this date is most likely correct, it cannot be confirmed.

The usual modifications were made in Macau to make the bus suitable for service conditions there, including the provision of full-depth sliding windows and a front

BELOW: Formerly EWY 422, L115 was the oldest of the post-war Bristol L5G's in Macau. Previously in the West Yorkshire fleet, it had the lower post-war Bristol PV2 radiator and higher profile ECW bodywork when seen here in April 1975. (Mike Davis

entrance which, together with that at the rear was fitted with swing gates. The rear sliding door was removed but in 1975, the recess into which it had once slid was still in evidence.

Despite this age group of ECW bodies having timber components in their construction, it had not by, 1975, been found necessary to replace major components such as main body frames or roof hoops. This was possibly due to the 1956 rebuild by West Yorkshire referred to above.

L116, L117 and L121
ex-Eastern Counties Omnibus Co Ltd

These three buses had chassis numbers 63.005, 63.068 and 63.197, all with low radiators and were all built in 1947, receiving new ECW timber-framed bodies. They were originally registered in England as FPW 514, FPW 519 and FPW 526, respectively.

These buses were purchased from Eastern Counties by dealer Ben Jordan in March 1963 (L116), December 1963 (L117) and March 1964 (L121), but it is believed that it was Norths who actually exported them. There is no known date of their export or arrival in Macau.

As with all other Bristol L5G's, the body was modified for local conditions in the usual manner with respect to window ventilation, an additional doorway and the provision of gates. In this rebuilt condition seating and layout was to B33FEXG,REXG.

By 1974

By 1974, each of these three chassis carried different body styles.

L116 (chassis 63.005) had a body rebuilt to the low profile pattern, loosely based on the pre-war ECW body-style—see L101 *et seq*, from which it differed only superficially, and had a PV2, low radiator.

L117 (chassis 63.068) retained its post-war pattern ECW body

ABOVE: Rebuilt—or rebodied—L116 opposite the Post Office in Macau's main street, Avenida de Almeida Ribeiro when photographed in April 1975 When in the UK this was FPW 514 in the Eastern Counties fleet. *(Mike Davis*

with high profile, unmodified to the extent that the recessed panel incorporating the last near-side window remained as it was when it lost the original external sliding door. Like L116 it became B33FEXG,REXG.

L121 (chassis 63.197) was originally as L117, but was partially rebuilt by "Fok Lei" in 1974 with a completely new nearside. The modified side had a front entrance and new centre exit. There was seating for 33— later reduced to B29FED,CED(sc) to accommodate a seated conductress. By using the original framework,

probably aluminium, "Fok Lei's" workshop retained an overall ECW appearance, especially as the front canopy and the flat upper side panels were not altered.

L121 was one of the first two yellow buses in the fleet and one of the the first to have the rear door repositioned in the centre—in both cases the other bus was L128 (*qv*).

Bridge Opening

L121, together with L118 and L128 (*qv*), opened the bus services across the Macau-Taipa Bridge in 1974.

LEFT: L117 was less drastically rebuilt than L116, above, and is still a distinctive Bristol/ECW product. As with some others of the type, the recess that once accommodated the sliding rear doorway can be seen clearly in this 1975 view. *(Mike Davis*

LEFT: L121 was, like L116 and L117, acquired from Eastern Counties and was originally similar. It had, however, by April 1975, received a completely new nearside, built by "Fok Lei", incorporating front and centre gateways; it, however retained its original offside. *(Mike Davis*

CENTRE LEFT: L121 as seen from the offside a few weeks later, in May 1975. *(Mike Davis*

L118, L119 & L120

ex-Bristol Omnibus Co Ltd

The buses that became "Fok Lei" L118, L119 and L120 were built in 1947 and were reportedly exported by Norths *circa* late 1960/early 1961 but would have made up one or more of the pairs of buses usually purchased, possibly not having been shipped all together. Another report states that all three reached Hong Kong by 1961 for trans-shipment to Macau.

These three were the only buses to have had dual entrances prior to their export to Macau. All were originally—and remained—33-seaters, the only difference being the gates, G, added by "Fok Lei" with whom they were B33FEXG,REXG

All UK-style side windows were replaced by full-depth sliding tropical style units. Both doorways had their sliding doors replaced by the isoteric Macau swing gates.

By 1974/75

L118—63.132 (JHT 848)—remained reasonably original and, in fact, was not converted to centre exit until 1980 but did operate with a seated conductress with its original front and crear doorways—fitted with gates.

L119—63.144 (JHT 852)—had, by 1974, been rebuilt extensively, probably after deterioration of the timber body frame in the high humidity of the climate affecting the South China coast

L120— 63.173 (JHT 863)—was rebodied in 1975, by Union Auto Body Builders, Kwai Chung, to the new 'standard' UABB pattern (*qv*).

L122

ex-Bristol Tramways

This bus came from a later sanction than L118-20, having chassis number 67.099, while the UK registration number was LHT 905.

According to the PSV Circle records it had entered service in 1948 as a Bristol L6B, that is with a Bristol AVW 6-cylinder engine. The bus was sold to North, the dealer, in January 1964 who removed the Bristol AVW engine and replaced it with a Gardner 5LW before exporting it. The familiar low-radiator was fitted from new.

Of interest was the fact that this bus was bodied when new by ECW, but in 1957 it received a 1950 vintage dual-purpose DP35R body by Bristol Body Works. This body was converted to *front* entrance B35F *bus* by Bristol to work OMO.

The UK-style sliding ventilators in the top of the side windows were retained and were of the BBW square cornered variety, although otherwise generally similar to contemporary ECW products—ECW used rubber-mounted, aluminium framed units. Below the sliding vents were additional full-depth sliding glasses and these were also fitted in windows which had no previoud vents.

A rear entrance was reinstated by "Fok Lei" and Macau-style swing gates were fitted at front and rear.

The BBW body was seen, and photographed, in 1975 when its registration number was M-10-87 but it is possible that this bus then carried the same number it was originally issued with in *circa* 1964 as a photograph of it was taken with that number in 1966.

L123 to Ll28

ex-United Automobile Services Ltd

These six buses were all built in 1949, and, with the exception of L128, all had the high profile ECW bodywork of post-war pattern. All were originally B35R when in United ownership, but underwant the usual metamorphosis to become B33FEXG,REXG in Macau. L128, which had a low profile body, was further rebuilt as described below.

L123. L124 and L127—chassis numbers 71.126, 71.176 and 79.037 (LHN 805/814/849) were all similar, both in outward appearance and mechanical detail, being Bristol L5G's with ECW bodies, having a Macau layout of B33FEXG,REXG

L125 and L126 had notable chassis, numbered 73.143R and 73.163R, the final 'R' standing for Rebuild. At the time of manufacture, severe restrictions were in place on the use of steel for certain key components in new bus production. After an operator's quota of new chassis had been completed, further acquisition of new buses could only be achieved in the form of 'Rebuilds' which were not subject to the same restrictions. Used running units were placed in new L-type chassis frames, and some even received new engines. L125, when new, had a Bristol AVW 6-cylinder engine, making it a Bristol L6B. United replaced the AVW in 1960 with a Gardner 5LW unit, thus changing the designation to L5G.

L128 was hardly the same bus as that built in 1948. It was fitted from new with a Bristol AVW 6-cylinder engine but was re-engined with a Gardner 5LW prior to

export. In 1974 a second-hand Gardner 5LW engine, bought form China Motor Bus, in Hong Kong, was fitted. The purpose was to impress the "Fok Lei" engineers with performance which could be obtained from 5LW engines when fully reconditioned.

The original ECW body was destroyed by fire in the Depot during May 1974 and replaced by "Fok Lei" who built a new body totheir simpler, low-profile design as used on L101, etc,and similar to L116. Thus by 1975 it differed in appearance to the other five buses bought from United Automobile at the same time and which were its contemporaries.

ABOVE: L125 was new with a BristolAVW 6-cylinder engine but this was replaced by a Gardner 5LW before export to Macau. *(David Withers*

BELOW: L126, seen here in April 1975, had previously been LHN 566 with UAS and had been in Macau for about eleven years. *(Mike Davis*

The doorway arrangement of L128, which had been altered in the usual "Fok Lei" manner, to become B33FEXG,REXG, was, when rebuilt in 1974, modified and, like L121, the rear doorway was moved to the central position. The same number of seats were retained —B33FEXG,CEXG— until the introduction of seated conductresses, together with power doors, when there was a reduction to B29FED,CXD(sc), but that belongs in a later section (*qv*).

The front dome was replaced by a flat fronted assembly, with flush destination screen glass. The chassis number was 79.042 and UK registration number was LHN 856.

BELOW: L128 was the victim of a depot fire and was rebodied by "Fok Lei" according to their 'standard' pattern, with the exception of a central doorway in place of a rear one. The canopy, too, was a development with a flat front and flush destination screen. *(Mike Davis*

LEFT: This 1966 photograph shows M-14-18 in largely original Macau condition and looking remarkably 'Tilling-like'. **Provided** that it had retained the same registration until 1974, *this **may** have been* the former United Automobile Services MHW 998 chassis number 79.127. *(H.Piercy*

BELOW: L129 (ex-MHW995 with Bristol Tramways) appears to be standing in a scrapyard but this was "Fok Lei's" only depot until 1976. Close examination reveals a brand new tyre on the front wheel, recently fitted. *(Mike Davis*

L129 and L130

ex-Bristol Tramways

These, the newest Bristol L5G's acquired by "Fok Lei", were of 1950 vintage with chassis numbers 79.107 and 79.127 respectively, having been registered MHW 995 and MHW 998 in the United Kingdom.

L129 and L130 had aluminium framed ECW bodywork, having been constructed after the final change to that material by ECW during 1949. Originally rear entrance with 35-seats, they became dual entrance, 33-seaters, like all the other L5G's which were not further rebuilt to centre exits.

LEFT: A 1978 view of L130 after it had been rearranged internally to accommodate a seated conductress. The trilingual signs for entrance and exit are evident in this view. *(J. Shearman*

Bristol-L's with various rebuilt or partly rebuilt bodies after 1981 - largely unidentifiable.

From 1975, most "Fok Lei" single-deck buses, including the Bristol L5G's, were rebuilt to enable them to operate with a seated conductress. Unfortunately, registration number swapping continued and with bodies undergoing drastic reconstruction, together with the demise of the fleet-numbering system, it became difficult, if not impossible, to ascertain which bus was which. As was the case prior to 1974, it was once again a case of saying that there is, for example, a Bristol L5G with a certain type of body, which, at a particular date, is carrying registration number such-and-such and not that such-and-such registration number always identifies a particular bus.

We therefore offer the reader a selection of photographs to illustrate the changes made without trying to be specific as to the actual chassis beneath a particular body.

The reason for the seated conductress was as a first step along a potentially dangerous political path towards one man operation—OMO.

TOP LEFT: L103 was still M-10-72 when seen in workshops during December 1981. The cab roof and canopy had been modified in a somewhat asymmetric manner. A new windscreen assembly had also been added, together with passenger doors in place of gates.
(Mike Davis

CENTRE LEFT: L105—see earlier photo—seen in November 1978 having been fitted with folding doors in place of the traditional swing gates.
(T. V. Runnacles

LOWER LEFT: This 1981 view of L121 was typical of the post-war L5G's with largely original bodies converted for seated conductress, and fitted with power-operated folding doors to the front 'ENTRADA' and central 'SAIDA'.

Bristol L5G's rebodied from 1975

During January 1975, two Bristol L5G chassis, 52.051 and 52.056, both of which had for some months—possibly two years or more—lain idle and in differing degrees of dereliction were sent to Hong Kong to be rebodied. Both had been new to West Yorkshire Road Car in 1941 where they were DWW 589 & DWW 590 respectively. Upon their return to Macau these two buses were fleet numbered L113 and L114 in chassis number order.

One of the pair had been stripped almost completely and was used as a shed in the 'old' depot yard while the other remained engineless but otherwise largely intact outside the same premises. Because the bodies had been stripped before John Shearman became part of the Company—and thus had access to the chassis number plates—it is not certain which of these two chassis was which.

General arrangement drawings were prepared by "Fok Lei" based on the design used for the two Albion EVK55CL single-deckers, VK 1 & VK2, a feature of which was the 'standee windows' above the main side windows—a feature that reflected the large numbers of standing passengers carried.

Each chassis was sent to a separate body builder, 'L113' going to Metro-Dodwell Motors and L114 going to Union Auto Body Builders who had built the aforementioned Albion bodies.

On completion, it was difficult to believe that both builders had been given the same set of drawings for, while UABB followed the design very closely, the result

of Metro-Dodwell's interpretation was a very angular body, even having a nearside front mudguard fabricated by welding and also of angular appearance.

L113 returned to Macau as B29FED,CXD and L114 as B31FED,CXD but by 1981 both were B32FED,CXD,sc.

ABOVE: This January 1975 view shows a Bristol L5G chassis at the bus station awaiting shipment to Sun Cheong in Hong Kong for rebodying. This is believed to be L110—chassis 50.088—despite the registration number from an LS5G, the date and lower radiator being the clues. *(John Shearman*

BELOW: L113 was, with L114 (centre) one of the first pair of L5G's to be sent to Hong Kong for rebodying. Each was sent to a different body builder; L113 going to Metro-Dodwell Motors who produced this somewhat angular result. L113 had returned to service only a few days brfore it was photographed in May 1975. *(Mike Davis*

36

ABOVE: L114, the second of the first two chassis sent to Hong Kong for rebodying, went to Union Auto Body Builders of Kwai Chung who had recently completed the bodies—to a similar design—on "Fok Lei's" two new Albion Viking chassis, VK 1 & VK 2. Both L113 and L114 had been new to West Yorkshire Road Car Co Ltd in 1941 and were thus nearly midway through their fourth decade of passenger service—with new bodies for years of further service. Both had high Bristol radiators. *(Mike*

The original high pre-war exposed radiators were retained at first but fibre-glass grilles were later fitted to conceal them.

Following the success of L114, further chassis were sent to UABB, those being L107 and L120—the latter with its lower radiator, also exposed at first.

BELOW: L120 was the fourth, and last, L5G to be rebodied in this UABB style and differed visually from L114 only by having a post-war, PV2, radiator, which however, was later concealed as shown on page 39. L120 was seen here in November 1977, the chassis—63.170—having been new to Bristol Tramways in 1947. *(David Withers*

Although there is nothing to suggest that the "Fok Lei"/UABB boody design was unsatisfactory, subsequent rebodies were to a more traditional outline, with curved bodysides and without 'standee-windows'. The author was informed by an employee of "Fok Lei" that these bodies were built by Sun Cheong, the contractor who later built the full-fronted bodies on L5G chassis (*qv*). These bodies had a layout of B31FED,CXD,sc and in 1981 seven such bodies were recorded, all with concealed radiators of various styles.

Buses rebodied from 1975

The L5G situation 1981-83

Half-cab bodies:

Fleet number	Regn. number	Body make
L107	M-19-56	UABB
L113	M-14-02	Dodwell
L114	M-16-04	UABB
L120	M-10-52	UABB
L110	M-20-74	Sun Choeng
L111	M-10-86	Sun Choeng
(L115?)	M-27-05	Sun Choeng
(L117?)	M-27-74	Sun Choeng
(L122?)	M-10-87	Sun Choeng
(L125?)	M-27-75	Sun Choeng
(L130?)	M-14-18	Sun Choeng

Full fronted bodies by Sun Cheong

Fleet number	Regn. number	
L105	M-19-07	
L109	M-11-19	
L112	M-14-10	
L116	M-29-83	Fleet numbers thus IF unchanged
L118	M-11-76	
L121	M-27-51	
L123	M-27-06	
L124	M-14-77	
L126	M-19-01	
L127	M-28-61	
L128	M-12-47	
L129	M-11-03	

ABOVE: L120 had been given a Lodekka-inspired concealed radiator grille by the time that this photograph was taken in June 1983. Also clearly visible is the "Fok Lei" bus stop showing that company's distinctive way of spelling 'ONIBUS'—this being a Portuguese colonial spelling and is the standard form in Brasil but without the preceding 'AUTO'. *(Mike Davis*

BELOW: As seen in this 1981 photograph, for a short time, L120 was fitted with the small radiator grille, similar to that of L110, above. Fortunately, the style seen left was chosen for most of the half-cab L5G's. *(Mike Davis*

Bristol L-type rebodied with full-fronted bodies

As the 1970's became the 1980's, "Fok Lei", in what might seem to have been a last-ditch attempt to keep its reliable and dependable Bristol L5G's on the road, sent a number of chassis for rebodying with the then current 'Hong Kong' style full-fronted bodywork, similar to that widely used regionally for school buses, often on Bedford and Isuzu forward-axle chassis and similar to the second batch of Albion Viking single-deck'ers and some of the Isuzus, both of which are described in this volume.

As has been repeatedly said, there is un-likely to be any connection between the registration numbers carried in 1974-75 and those carried after rebodying. The only thing that can be certain is that a certain chassis was carrying a new body. Unfortunately the chassis numbers were not recorded when rebodying occurred. On arrival back in Macau, any old number may have been allocated.

TOP RIGHT: M-14-18 may well be the original L130, the least old L5G to arrive in Macau. It had been rebodied in Hong Kong to a style similar to that used for the later full-fronted rebodies. The style incorporates some features of the UABB body—front wing particularly—while the remainder of the body resembles the products of Sun Cheong and Wong Ming. This photograph shows the bus with a small cowl and grille concealing the low radiator—a style also carried by L120 for a short while prior to its being replaced by the style on the previous page. *(Ian Lynas*

CENTRE: This view of the bus at that time carrying the registration M-11-76 shows off well the attractive lines of a vehicle that started life with a post-war ECW half-cab body. In this June 1983 view, even without passengers, the rear springs appear 'tired'. Note the trouble taken to provide a neat replacement 'Bristol' badge. *(Mike Davis*

LOWER RIGHT: Another view of a similarly rebodied Bristol L5G, this time in October 1982. Here the bus has its folding passenger doors closed and is carrying a full load, depressing the rear springs further than those depicted above. *(Mike Davis*

Austin —single-deck buses

At one time, probably until the late 1960's, "Fok Lei" operated two buses with forward-control Austin chassis fitted diesel engines and five-speed gearboxes. They were identical to each other and about 27ft 6in long, normal for 1950-60, in which period they may have been built.

"Fok Lei" purchased the chassis new in about 1960 and then, possibly in their own workshops, built timber-framed bodies very closely modelled on the final design of pre-war ECW body as fitted to Bristol L5G's. The only significant difference in appearance was that the two Austins were full-fronted, with an enclosed radiator. The panels above the side windows immediately curved over the roof without an intervening flat panel as on post-war ECW single-deck bodies. There was a single-piece, rectangular, back window, a front destination box—but none at the back—of ECW style. Tubular metal swing gates of "Fok Lei" design and manufacture were fitted at both the front and rear doorways

Both buses were sold to COMPANHIA DE AUTO-OMNIBUS DE TAIPA, on Taipa Island and in 1974 passed to the new restructured islands operator, CTPEMI.

Vehicle Specification: Austin	
Chassis:	Austin export PSV chassis
Engine:	Austin 51JU/1188JA
Gearbox:	BMC 5-speed manual
Body make:	Fok Lei.
Body layout:	FB33FEX,REX,G.
Date built:	circa 1960
Total:	2
Length:	27ft 6in
Width:	7ft 6in
Height:	10ft
Wheelbase:	?

Austin—fleet list		
Regn number	Chassis number	Engine number
M-13-61	214140	51JU/1188JA/D753
M-25-50	?	51JU/1188JA/D742

BELOW: No good photographs of the Austins have been located which were taken while they were in service with "Fok Lei". The reader is thus directed to the section describing the buses of Auto Carros de Taipa and CTPEMI as the Austins were transferred to those fleets without much external alteration—save two changes of colour scheme. The only photograph to show that the Austins once worked in Macau City is in the postcard reproduced below where a solitary Austin can be seen to the left of centre, close to the wharf, outside the company's head office—ringed. The causeway in the background joins mainland China with one of its off-shore islands, left. Despite appearances, Macau does indeed drive on the left. There are two separate main roads in the picture, one to service the wharfs and the other, nearer to the camera, is the main road. The bus station is at the centre of the picture. *(John Shearman collection*

Beadle-Bedford—New to Eastern National

Overshadowed by the dominance of the forty Bristols, the fleet of nine Beadle-Bedfords represented virtually a fifth of the total of 49 second-hand single-deck buses obtained from the UK by "Fok Lei". The withdrawal of the last of these Beadle-Bedfords in 1976 (possibly 1977) prior to the demise of any of the Bristols, has also led to their often being passed-over by those interested in Macau's buses.

This is a pity, as in some ways these unusual buses were of even greater interest than the Bristols, not only because of their comparative rarity but because of their overall design and construction concept. One might have thought that they were not suitable candidates for export both because of their lightweight build and their not having been designed for a long life. When purchased by Tilling/BTC operators, they were intended to be not much more than a stopgap measure at a time of vehicle shortage, although their merit in being economical buses to operate was always recognised.

Little has been written and published to describe the chassisless buses—and the later coaches—built by John C.

Vehicle Specification—Beadle-Bedford	
Chassis:	Mechanical components from new Bedford OB-type integrated into a Beadle-built chassisless body
Engine:	Gardner 4LK
Gearbox:	Manual gearbox and clutch
Body make:	J. C. Beadle Ltd
Date new:	1946 (BB148) or 1949—remainder
Date to Macau:	1962/63
Total	9:
Length:	27ft 6in —all dimensions nominal
Width:	7ft 6in
Wheelbase:	?

Beadle but soon after World War II, Beadle took their post-war chassis mounted bus body, designed to resemble the Tilling Group's standard outline, a big step forward by developing it into a complete, integrally built semi-chassisless bus. Into the resultant buses, mechanical units were fitted, in some cases, salvaged from pre-war buses then being scrapped or, in other instances, new units supplied by outside bus chassis manufacturers.

The lightweight chassisless buses built by Beadle in the 1945 to 1950 period—the coaches came later—are thus of considerable significance and historic importance.

Four prototypes, followed by only 109 in the production run–plus one van–of these vertical engined, full-fronted, rear-entrance buses were built, so they were hardly common-place. (There were also some others developed in association with Sentinel but these differed in that they were underfloor engined with front entrances.)

Eastern National was selected to take delivery of the first and third prototypes of 1945 and 1946 respectively. The first was fitted with Commer running units but of interest here was the third which was Bedford equipped, being registered LNO 150. Presumably this was well received as, in 1949, nine of the production vehicles entered the same fleet. All ten of them survived in service with Eastern National until 1960.

Their Bedford running units included the 3.5 litre, 6-cylinder petrol engines of the type fitted to Bedford OB buses and coaches. However, for reasons of economy, the petrol engines were soon replaced by Gardner 4LK diesel engines, this occurring in 1951/2, during their time with Eastern National. The Bedford 4-speed crash gearbox, axles, etc. were retained to the end.

Nine of the ten, including the prototype LNO 150, were sold to A.M.C.C. of Frating, Essex—some without seats—circa late 1961. The

ABOVE: LNO 150, the prototype for the Beadle buses with Bedford OB running units, seen here in its Eastern National condition. *(Peter Shearman*
BELOW: One of the 'production' buses and the only one of the Eastern National ten that did not pass to "Fok Lei", Macau. Note that the front had a less pronounced curve and a raised destination box.*(John Shearman*

BEADLE-BEDFORD Fleet list as 1974—BB141-149

Chassisless vehicle number	Bedford mechanical unit no.	Year built	UK regn number	Body layout at export	Date registered in Macau	Macau fleet number	July 1974 Macau reg. no.	Later regn. number	Notes
JCB ?	?	1949	NVX ?	FB35R	08.02.62	BB141	M-15-77	-	Withdrawn 6/75
JCB ?	?	1949	NVX ?	FB35R	?	BB142	M-16-71	-	Scrapped 1974
JCB ?	?	1949	NVX ?	FB35R	?	BB143	M-19-30	-	Scrapped 1973
JCB 74	OB97068	1949	NVX 531	FB35R	17.08.62	BB144	M-19-31	M-20-74—from 5/75	Withdrawn 9/75
JCB 44	OB95555	1949	NVX 525	FB35R	?	BB145	M-19-54	-	Scrapped ?73/74
JCB 76	OB186285	1949	NVX533	FB35R	25.09.62	BB146	M-19-56	-	Withdrawn 6/75—Regn. no. to L107
JCB ?	?	1949	NVX ?	FB35R	16.04.63	BB147	M-20-72	-	Converted to lorry 1977
JCB 3	OB36532	1946	LNO 150	FB33R	16.04.63	BB148	M-20-73	-	Withdrawn ?76/77
JCB ?	?	1949	NVX ?	FB35R	16.04.63	BB149	M-20-74	-	Withdrawn 5/75—Regn. no. to L110

All new to Eastern National Omnibus Company Limited.

BELOW: By July 1973, when this photograph was taken at Barra, the vehicle then carrying number M-16-71 was the only Beadle-Bedford which retained the original frontal 'drooping' windows. The exact identity of this 1949 bus was not detectable as it was one of those which had by that time lost its vehicle number plate. By January 1974 it was out of use; by June 1974 it had been scrapped. In the background is another of the Beadle-Bedfords; it will be noted that the 'drooping' rear windows were retained, as they were on all other buses of this type, together with (painted-out) rear destination screens. *(John Shearman*

odd one was sold elsewhere a few months later. At that stage, these lightweight buses had already achieved a lifespan as long as many contemporary heavyweight Bristol L-types were allowed and with the large quantities of these and other buses then available on the second-hand market, it would have seemed almost inevitable that the nine Beadle-Bedfords would have had only one fate—scrap.

Surprisingly, this was not to be; surprise turns to near astonishment that such buses as these should find an export customer and one whose demands on them would be for heavy duty service and with the expectation of their providing many more years of intensive further use. Admittedly, their Gardner engines were an attraction but these would have been readily saleable on the world market, in or removed from the vehicles. In terms of passenger/miles, the already achieved full-lifespan of these nine buses had hardly started!

"Fok Lei" purchased all nine of those available,

probably not all as one batch, in which case one may suppose that early experience with the first one, or more, was favourable so that the remainder were acquired. It is also noteworthy that these quaint buses were purchased not before or after the Bristol L5G fleet was being expanded but at the same time.

In Macau, they had the usual front doorway cut into the saloon behind the bulkhead—this despite their integral construction—and retained the original rear entrance

The 'J.C.B.' and 'OB' vehicle number plates remained in one vehicle in 1974 but was 'preserved' by a person unknown before it could be recovered officially.

On arrival in Macau, all had Beadle's 'drooping' windscreens, cab side windows and back windows. Beadle buses differed from later coaches in profile, by having straight waistlines, whereas those on the coaches were downswept to the rear.

RIGHT: This March 1975 photograph shows the prototype Beadle-Bedford, originally LNO 150, as it was after modifications by "Fok Lei", particularly the provision of a raised front destination box. As this was an addition the upper surface of the box did not join the top of the roof in a continuous flat plane, instead there was a small 'hump' which careful study will allow readers to detect. The more curved lines of front corner pillars are apparent but the squared-off windscreen and cab side-windows were common to most of the other buses of this type after some years in Macau. (Mike Davis

LOWER RIGHT: For comparison, this photograph shows one of the 1949 'production' batch of Beadle-Bedfords in the form of Fok Lei BB143 parked at Barra on the 27th May 1975, day on which the four double-deckers, LD205/6 and PD207/8, arrived in Macau from UABB in Hong Kong. The different destination box and front corner contours can be readily seen in this view. (Mike Davis

By July 1973, just one of the eight surviving Beadles (one that had lost its vehicle number plate) retained its original windscreens—which curved downwards and outwards from a central pillar—and the cab side windows which accordingly also sloped downwards towards the front. The other seven had all been rebuilt by "Fok Lei" with 'squared-up' windscreens and cab side windows, all of which followed the line of the side waist rail.

When built these buses had rear entrances, with sliding doors, but, as with the Bristol L's, the door was removed and an additional front entrance was added by "Fok Lei" in the first bay behind the bulkhead, together with standard Macau-style gates. All seated 33 passengers in Macau service.

Externally, the single-line indicator above the back windows remained in situ, albeit painted-over, together with the hinged and flared skirt panels, often to be seen flying loose as a bus swept left or right around a corner. The original radiator grille design survived as did the raised front destination boxes.

The 1946 prototype, LNO 150, was built with a more curved front, two, flush, single-line, destination indicators and other detail differences. For its use in Macau, a raised destination box was added but, unlike the 1949-built

examples, the top of this did not continue straight into the roof line, there being a shallow but distinctive 'hump' at the point of joining. Careful examination of photographs will reveal this point.

Internally, the luggage racks, built-in lights and the original meagre and austere seats were retained.

All nine entered service in Macau in 1962/3. The British registration of JCB3 was LNO 150, and the other nine were NVX 525-33 (NVX529 being the only one not exported). When fleet numbered in 1974, these nine buses became the BB class and were allocated BB141-9 in order of entering service—and, for completeness, included BB142/3/5 which were scrapped the previous year. Although allocated, none of the nine survived to carry a fleet number, the last being withdrawn in 1976 or 1977.

These amazing little buses lasted 25-years and longer, in active service, the most arduous period of which were in the twilight of their lives—three times more than reckoned and, even then, one was further extended as a lorry. If we take the prototype—built in 1946—which was one of the last two to be withdrawn, the total period served was 30years!!! Even then it was due to a lack of spare parts, rather than any structural weakness, that resulted in their final withdrawal, despite the constant overloading—sometimes gross overloading and spirited driving over some fearfully potholed roads.

Lorry - Amazingly, the withdrawn hulk of BB147 (M-20-72) was extracted from a line of withdrawn BB's in 1977 and was converted to an open backed lorry, in replacement of the ex-military Austin Loadstar whose registration number, M34-64, it took. This unidentified JCB had thus been saved once from certain scrapping in the UK and was then saved yet again from a Macau scrapyard

RIGHT and LOWER RIGHT: The amazing conversion of a chassisless bus to an open-backed lorry. One is tempted to ask how the necessary rigidity and strength was achieved! This remarkable vehicle had previously been BB147 (M-20-72) but upon its conversion, it took the registration of the small Austin 'Loadstar' military lorry that it superseded, M-34-64. *(Both by John Shearman*

Morris —single-deck buses

The history of these four Morris chassis is similar to that of the two Austins (*page 41*). It is probable, however, that they were bodied later than the Austins, because the bodywork resembles that of the Beadle chassisless buses which were obtained in 1962.

The bodies were said to have been built in Kowloon, Hong Kong, by Sun Cheong Auto Body Builders, although it has not been possible to confirm this. The obvious conclusion to make is that Sun Cheong modelled the bodies of the four Morris's from the Beadle-Bedford's design and, apart from having a conventional chassis and chrome grille, there were few visual differences between them and the Beadle-Bedfords (*page 42*).

The body design was very reminiscent of the Beadles but there were, of course, differences but these were of detail rather than total concept. The windscreens were 'squared' in the style to which "Fok Lei" rebuilt most of the Beadle-Bedfords. The two-piece back windows of the Sun Cheong bodies were also squared and did not droop—as did the Beadles—and they did not have a back destination box.

Internally, there was more woodwork around the window frames although the fixtures seemed to be very 'British'.

As on the Austins, the dual entrances were fitted with swing gates designed and made by "Fok Lei" and the body layout was FB33FEXG,REXG.

Morris—fleet list

Regn number	Chassis number
M-12-18	?
M-12-19	51771
M-12-56	?
M-12-57	?

Three, at least, were sold to Lo Wan Lee On bus company on Coloane island. Of these, two remained in passenger service in 1977; one was derelict, while a fourth was still to be seen in Macau, converted to a lorry, but it is not known if it also was originally sold to Coloane.

One of the Morris chassis numbers, that of M-12-19, is believed to have been 51771 and from this, the information in the above specification 'box' is offered.

BELOW: This is the only known photograph of one of the four Morris buses when with "Fok Lei". It is seen here in 1966, waiting on the stand at the bus station, near the pier for the river boat to China, awaiting its next duty on Route 4. Other illustrations of these buses with bodywork copied from the style of the Beadle-Bedfords can be found in a later section detailing the Coloane bus operator (Lo Wan Lee On) and CTPEMI. It is stressed that these buses most certainly did have a conventional chassis. Interestingly, and assuming that there was no number-swapping, this bus M-12-57, was the one of its type not to survive to become part of the CTPEMI fleet in 1974, having by then been converted to a lorry. *(Ron Phillips collection*

Bristol LS single-deckers

There is less use of the qualifiers 'possibly', 'probably' and 'maybe' and more feeling of 'certainty' when describing the buses that, in 1974, were grouped together as the LS-class, than there was with the Bristol L5G's. Fortunately every LS in Macau had retained its body number intact so that a positive identity could be established.

Following the last Bristol L5G's, "Fok Lei" acquired ten underfloor engined Bristol LS single-deckers from a variety of operators, between 1969 and 1974. Three, all from West Yorkshire Road Car, had originally been built as dual-purpose vehicles with high-backed seats and additional trim, while the remainder were purely buses with seats to match.

The first two LS5G's, which entered Macau service in 1969, were converted by "Fok Lei" into a two-doorway arrangement; the original opposite the driver, plus a new one cut into the bay behind the rear wheel-arch. All eight subsequent deliveries, however had three doorways—the two as above plus a centre doorway behind the front wheel-arch. Although their front-most doorway was often unused until the introduction of passenger-flow during the late 1970's, these buses must have been amongst the few British domestic-style three entrance buses in the world!.

Two nearside seats, one ahead of the rear doorway and the one behind the centre doorway were relocated longitudinally as a consequence of these extra doorways. The two, two-doorway LS5G's having a capacity of 43+12 while the remaining eight with three doorways became 39+12.

All LS5G's had the horizontally mounted Gardner 5HLW diesel engine and manually operated crash gearboxes with conventional clutch.

By virtue of their chassis type 'LS', when the fleet was numbered in 1975, the prefix for these ten buses became LS and all were allocated fleet numbers in the sequence of entering service in Macau but by 1978 not all buses actually carried those numbers. Although registration numbers were fairly static, it should not be assumed that there were *no* number swaps at all.

Vehicle Specifications: Bristol LS5G	
Chassis:	Bristol LS5G.
Engine:	Gardner 5HLW, horizontal underfloor.
Gearbox:	5-speed manual
Brakes:	Vacuum-servo (triple-servo system)
Body make:	ECW - much rebuilt by Fok Lei.
Body layout:	B43+12T or B39+12T—various later rearrangements
Date built:	1953-56
Regd. in Macau:	1969-73.
Length: 30ft	Width: 8ft
	Height: 10ft 1in (laden)

The Bristol LS—Light Saloon—was introduced in 1951 and was a joint production of Bristol and Eastern Coachworks in which the body formed an integral part of the complete vehicle. The design was not 'chassisless' in the sense that the running units were attached directly to the body structure as in some other designs and the existence of a complete, albeit flimsy, chassis frame simplified the construction process as, with suitable additional bracing, the chassis could be driven under its own power from the Bristol chassis factory, in the West Country, to ECW at Lowestoft on the opposite side of England, on the East Anglian coast. (TOWNSIN A: BUSES AND TRAMS 1953) Thus, strictly speaking this was a Bristol/ECW vehicle. It is thus interesting to discover the extent to which the bodies were altered by "Fok Lei"—from cutting open the side to accommodate a centre doorway within the wheelbase, to almost completely rebuilding the body structure.

ABOVE: LS139 was the last but one LS to enter service with "Fok Lei", having been acquired in 1974. It had started life with United Automobile Services along with Macau sister vehicles LS131 & LS132, having been sold by UAS at the same time, but, unlike the latter, LS139 passed first to Thames Valley Traction Co before export to the Far East. This 1975 photograph shows the almost original destination screens but also the additional two passenger entrances but no front door. *(Mike Davis*

BRISTOL LS5G		Fleet list as fleet numbered 1974—LS131-L140							
Chassis number	Year chassis built	UK regn number	Col. 4	Body at export:			Date to UK dealer or* registered	Macau fleet number	July 1974 Macau reg. no.	Notes
				make	number	layout				
97.129	1953	SHN 727	UAS	ECW	6775-2	B45F	18.08.69	LS131	M-38-10	
89.071	1952	PHN 848	UAS	ECW	5722-2	B45F	29.09.69	LS132	M-38-80	
93.025	1953	LWR 434	WY	ECW	5727-2	DP41F	02.09.70	LS133	M-44-29	
107.074	1955	OXW 152	WY	ECW	8229-2	DP41F	03.11.70	LS134	M-45-77	
89.112	1952	UHT 493	BT	ECW	6858-2	B45F	03.11.71	LS135	M-53-81	Built with Commer TS3 two-stroke diesel engine
101.140	1954	PHW 938	BT	ECW	6848-2	B45F	15.12.71*	LS136	M-55-40	
105.103	1954	PHW 947	BTH	ECW	6857-2	B45F	11.02.72*	LS137	M-31-05	
117.049	1956	RWW 982	WY	ECW	8929-2	B45F	31.03.72*	LS138	M-58-23	Built as DP41F
97.130	1953	SHN 728	UAS	ECW	6776-2	B45F	17.01.74*	LS139	M-11-43	
105.006	1954	PHW 940	BT	ECW	6850-2	B45F	06.03.74*	LS140	M-18.05	

Key to Column 4: Principal UK operator: BT: Bristol Tramways & Carriage Co. UAS: United Automobile Services BTH: Bath Tramways WY: West Yorkshire Road Car Co.

LS131, 132 and 139

ex-United Automobile Services Ltd

These three basically similar buses were acquired over a long period. LS131 entered service in August 1969, and LS132 in September 1969, but LS139 did not join them until 1974 having been operated by Thames Valley from 1968 to 1973.*

Built in 1953, 1952 and 1953 respectively, they carried chassis numbers 97.129. 89.071 and 97.130, having originally been registered SHN 727, PHN 848 and SHN 728—LS131 and 139, it will be noticed, had consecutive chassis and UK registration numbers.

LS131 and 132 retained the original front entrance but "Fok Lei" added an additional rear entrance, behind the rear axle, while LS139 had three entrances, two of which were as on LS131 and 132, with a second additional entrance behind the front axle. All had gates, except the original front entrance on LS139, which appeared to have neither gate nor door, being protected only by a thin metal chain.

LS131 and 132 were B41FEXG,REXG, while LS139 was B41FEX,CEXG,REXG— no front gate or door—and retained its original three-part destination/route/number screens, but only the large intermediate route box was used.

*SOURCE : PSV CIRCLE HISTORY OF UNITED AUTOMOBILE SERVICES.

BELOW: Although M-38-10 had been fleet numbered LS131 on paper for nearly a year it had not been applied to the bus when it was photographed early in 1975. Before export, this bus had been SHN 727 in the United Automobile Services fleet. *(Mike Davis*

RIGHT: M-38-80 was LS132 but not for nearly two years after it was photographed here in January 1973. The original three part destination screens had long since given way to this single screen arrangement set in the original large destination box. Like its sister, then M-38-10, above, it had only one additional doorway. *(E. L. Rees*

LS133, LS134, and LS138

ex-West Yorkshire Road Car Co Ltd

Originally registered LWR 434, OWX 152 and RWW 982, LS133, 134 and 138 were built in 1953, 1955 and 1956 respectively and had chassis numbers 93.025, 107.074 and 117.049.

They were built as 41-seat dual purpose vehicles for semi-express services in and around Yorkshire, these three were subsequently rebuilt as 45 seat saloons by ECW although two of them managed to retain some of the decorative beading and the rear bumpers associated with the dual purpose semi-coaches. LS133 and 134 arrived in Macau in 1970 and LS138 in March 1972. LS133 lacked the bodyside decorative beading found on the other former two

but otherwise the outward appearance of all these three former West Yorkshire LS's was similar.

The original two part destination screens were retained, but the glass of the number box was painted out. During their early years in Macau, they were all modified by fitting two additional entrances, one behind each nearside wheel-arch. On LS 133 and 138, the original front doors were removed, consequently having neither gates nor doors, while the centre and rear entrances had gates. On LS134, however, the original front folding door was retained but usually remained out of use. The bodies were DP41F in England but became B39FEX(D*),CEXG,REXG—or B39T in PSV Circle terms—although the front doorway was not in regular use. (*D on LS134 only.)

RIGHT: LS133 standing in front of the "Fok Lei" head office in March 1975. This former West Yorkshire 'express' or 'dual-purpose' vehicle (LWR 434) had lost its distinctive beading, or moulding, but the destination screens were as original. The additional centre and rear doorways were added by "Fok Lei". *(Mike Davis*

BELOW: Sister vehicle, LS134, seen here at Barra in May 1975. This former express vehicle (OXW 152) had retained most of its decorative beading on the front and sides and had also acquired two additional doorways—gateways to be precise. *(Mike Davis*

ABOVE: This picture shows the rear of LS134 being refuelled from the oil company's tanker in the street at Barra terminus. To be seen in the background are the two Daimler CVG6's that had recently arrived from Hong Kong by barge and, in the right foreground, L104X, the Bristol L5G breakdown crane. *(Mike Davis*

LEFT: The third of the former 'dual-purpose' or 'Express' bodied LS5G's was "Fok Lei" LS138 which is seen here outside the Company office at the bus station. *(Mike Davis*

LS135, 136 and 140

ex-Bristol Tramways

LS135, 136 and 140 originally carried UK registration numbers LWR 434, OWX 152 and RWW 982, and were built in 1953, 1955 and 1956 respectively. LS135 was originally B43D and LS136 and 140 were built as B45F. In Macau, however, they all became three-entrance buses with a seating capacity of 39.

LS135 was most unusual in that it was given a two-stroke Commer TS3 diesel engine when built in 1952. It is thus possible that the original classification of the chassis (89.112) was LS3C, or even LSX3C, as experimental Bristols sometimes had an additional X. By the time that LS135 arrived in Macau, a Gardner 5HLW engine, number 103 014, had been fitted.

LS136 was the first Bristol LS to be refurbished by "Fok Lei", the first to be given the new yellow livery, and the first to carry a fleet number. It was intended that LS136 would be a relief for the two Albion Vikings, VK1 and VK2, bought new in 1975 and initially allocated to the cross-bridge routes, until double-deck buses became available for those prestigious services. LS136, thereafter, operated normal city routes.

The door layout, once triple, was reduced to dual, ie, front and centre, with remotely controlled manual gates. The front gate was worked by the driver through a series of levers while the centre exit was controlled similarly by the seated conductress.

LS135 was subsequently rebuilt in a similar manner to LS133 with centre and rear entrance only.

52

LS137—ex-Bath Tramways

Apart from coming from a different operator, LS137 was almost identical to LS135/6 which came from Bristol Tramways, the parent company of Bath Tramways. The body layout was altered to three entrances and 39 seats. The British registration number was PHW 947 and the chassis number 105.103.

BELOW: LS137 was parked outside the bus station in April 1975, having arrived in Macau in 1972. It was new to Bath Tramways as PHW 947 in 1954. *(Mike Davis*

Bristol LS5G buses rebuilt during the latter 1970's

Before the introduction of one man operation (OMO), at least two LS's had their front entrances panelled-over, leaving, in one case, the centre and rear entrances and, in the other, introducing two entrances between the front and rear wheels. Both remained in this condition until withdrawn.

When the idea of eventual conversion to one-man-operation was finally accepted, the standard arrangement on the LS-class utilized the front doorway as an entrance plus a centre or, strictly speaking, forward, exit. Fares were paid into a farebox beside the driver. In fact, the LS's were among the few second-hand "Fok Lei" buses that were suitable for one-man-operation

By 1978, registration number swapping had spread to the LS5G's and it is impossible to follow any further the fortunes of a particular chassis with certainty. The remaining story is told by reference to photographs

LEFT: This LS with its front entrance doorway removed provides a good example of registration number swapping between vehicles when in workshops for protracted periods. This is very definitely not the express bodied LS5G that had carried registration M-45-77 in previous pictures as LS134. Compare this door arrangement with that on the next page. (The front entrance was later reinstated while that at the rear was removed—the centre doorway was retained as the exit.) *(John Shearman*

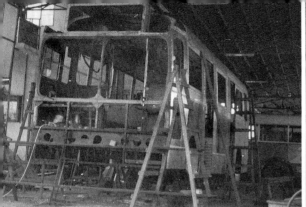

ABOVE and ABOVE RIGHT: During June 1977 an anonymous LS5G was seen in the new workshops with two doorways between the axles. Front entrances had proved unpopular with drivers, so the front doorway was panelled over. To encourage successful passenger flow operation, with a seated-conductress, two doorways were provided within the wheelbase. (This was less satisfactory later when driver-only operation was introduced.) These pictures also highlight the extent of rebuilding undertaken by "Fok Lei" workshop staff—the skeleton of another bus body-frame can be clearly seen. *(John Shearman*

RIGHT: The same vehicle seen in service in 1982, having acquired the registration number M-31-05. It had also acquired twin headlights which may or may not have been necessary for Macau conditions. *(John Shearman*

RIGHT and LOWER RIGHT: Two examples of relatively unaltered bodywork adapted for front-entrance-centre exit, passenger-flow operation by panelling-over the rear doorway. There is reason to believe that at least the upper of the two, the 'Express' bodied M-44-29 was the original LS133. There is less certainty about the bus carrying M-53-81. *(Both Mike Davis*

TOP LEFT: M-38-10 with rebuilt front dome and fitted with new stainless-steel swing gates in 1976.
(John Shearman

CENTRE LEFT: The same bus in 1981 fitted with power-operated folding doors.
(Mike Davis

BELOW: M-11-43, seen here in December 1981 having been thoroughly rebuilt and with power doors to the front entrance and centre exit. This was the style adopted for most of the rebuilds and it is believed that all were treated to some extent, although this cannot be confirmed. *(Mike Davis*

Albion single-deck buses—1975-series—New to "Fok Lei"

These two buses were the first to have been bought new by "Fok Lei" since the Austins and Morrises and had chassis identical to those of the 100 Duple Dominant bodied coaches delivered to neighbouring Kowloon Motor Bus during 1975—in fact, they were diverted from that order, which was extended by two.

In view of their being purchased new, these two buses were given fleet numbers outside the main fleet numbering scheme—VK1 & VK2 (M-85-79 and M-85-80) with chassis numbers 51711A and 51711B of the EVK55CL type. In Albion language that means Export, Viking, 55 (denoting twin line full air brakes), C (denoting fourth major design change since introduction), L (long wheelbase). They were powered by the Leyland 0.401 diesel engine, driving the rear wheels through a five-speed constant mesh Albion GB255 gearbox. The two chassis arrived in Hong Kong late in 1974 and were sent to what became Union Auto Body Builders at Sai Yee Street, Kowloon, to receive the "Fok Lei" designed bodywork. This very soundly prepared design had seats for 43 passengers, as originally built and dual doors; one in front of the front axle, and the other ahead of the rear axle in anticipation of operation with a seated conductress (then still to be agreed with the trade union, and eventually introduced in September 1975). The

Vehicle Specification: Albion Vikings VK1 & 2	
Chassis:	Leyland (Albion) Viking EVK55CL
Engine:	Leyland E0.401
Gearbox:	GB255 5-speed constant-mesh.
Body make:	Union Auto Body Builders, Hong Kong.
Date introduced:	11th February 1975.
Total:	2
Length:	31ft 8in 9650mm
Width:	8ft 2½in 2500mm
Height:	10ft 6in 3200mm — nominal
Wheelbase:	16ft 1in 4900mm

seating was reduced to 38 + 17 for seated conductress operation and the front and centre doorways were designated as entrance and exit respectively. Power operated jack-knife doors were fitted to both doorways.

When new, VK1 & VK2 were allocated to cross-bridge route 11 to Taipa, as Fok Lei's two-bus contribution to that route, pending the introduction of double-deckers, at which time they were transferred to Route 3 which served the hydrofoil and ferry piers—also a two vehicle route.

RIGHT and BELOW: Nearside and offside views of the first two Albion Vikings delivered new to "Fok Lei" in 1975. The only disappointment in UABB's interpretation of the Fok Lei prepared general arrangement drawings was the disproportionately small front grille which it was intended should have been much larger by means of it boasting a wider surround, similar to that applied to Albions of the subsequent, 1981, batch. However, the standee windows were faithfully incorporated as per the drawings. *(Both photos by Mike Davis)*

Albion Single-deck buses—1981-series—New to "Fok Lei"

The first two Vikings, VK1 & VK2 proved to be extremely reliable, being of durable build. They were also economical to operate—the only unfortunate 'note' being the squealing brakes which taxed many an engineer's ingenuity in resolving on the similar EVK55CL's in Kowloon. It was, therefore, not surprising that two larger repeat orders were placed with Metro Dodwell Motors of Kowloon for six, followed by a further nine Albions.

All fifteen Vikings were delivered during 1981, the last entering service in early 1982. They were based on a similar chassis type to those purchased in 1975 but with minor developments giving DL and EL suffixes to the EVK55 model number.

The first six chassis are believed to have been a diverted order (Cyprus?) while the remaining nine were ordered direct from Leyland Motors. In both cases the engine remained the Leyland E0.401 as in the earlier VK1 and VK2.

All fifteen buses were bodied by Sun Cheong to a design, not unlike that used by the builder to rebody the Bristol L5G's, although seating was reduced to 23—B23FE,CX,OMO—in order to provide more space for standees. The layout provided for a front entrance, ahead of the axle, a seated conductress and a centre exit. The layout was later revised to B38FE,CX,OMO.

Chassis numbers from MA-90-42 onwards differed from previous deliveries in being entirely numeric—no suffix letter—as these were built at Bathgate after the Albion plant had ceased to build complete chassis.

As had become the practice by 1981 no fleet numbers were allocated to these vehicles which were known solely by their MA-prefixed registration numbers.

Vehicle Specification: Albion Vikings—1981		
Chassis:	Leyland (Albion) Viking EVK55EL & EVK55DL	
Engine:	Leyland E0.401	
Gearbox:	Leyland 5-speed constant-mesh.	
Body make:	Sun Cheong, Hong Kong	
Body layout:	B23FE,CX,D,sc+multi-standees; later B38D	
Date introduced:	1981-82	
Total:	15	
Length:	31ft 8in	9650mm
Width:	8ft 2½in	2500mm
Height:	10ft 6in	3200mm — nominal
Wheelbase:	16ft 1in	4900mm

Albion Viking EVK55

Fleet number	Regn. number	Chassis number	Date introduced
EVK55CL			
UNION AUTO BODIES—B43D			
VK1	M-85-79	51711A	2/75
VK2	M-85-80	51711B	2/75
EVK55DL			
SUN CHEONG BODIES—B38D			
-	MA-69-72	?	1981
-	MA-69-73	?	1981
-	MA-69-74	?	1981
-	MA-69-75	?	1981
-	MA-82-14	?	1981
-	MA-82-15	?	1981
EVK55EL			
SUN CHEONG BODIES—B38D			
-	MA-90-42	569563	11.81
-	MA-90-43	569565	11.81
-	MA-92-45	569610	11.81
-	MA-92-46	569611	11.81
-	MA-92-24	570332	12.81
-	MA-94-25	570333	12.81
-	MA-94-26	570334	12.81
-	MA-94-27	570335	12.81
-	MA-94-28	570336	12.81

ABOVE LEFT: MA-90-43 had been in service barely a month when photographed on 20th December 1981. *(Mike Davis)*

LEFT: From the first of the two 1981 Albion batches, MA-82-15 displays the body design shared by Albions, Isuzus and rebodied Bristol L5G's. It was standing in bright December sunshine in 1981 when seen here. *(Mike Davis)*

The Double-Deck Buses from 1975

As a consequence of the Leal Senado urging "Fok Lei" to improve its service as a requirement for the renewal of the franchise, the Company commissioned a British transport management consultant to effect necessary changes. In part, he turned to the traditional British double-decker, perhaps not a surprising move as he was known as a staunch protagonist of the species for selected overseas use.

Hindsight was a welcome ally and, having witnessed the problems which both China Motor Bus and Kowloon Motor Bus had experienced with second-hand, rear engined Atlanteans under Hong Kong conditions, the choice naturally fell in favour of front engined types, most preferred being those with a Gardner engine. Unfortunately, however, as described on page 12, supplies of the desired Bristols were not good and neither were there many other front-engined double-deckers on the second-hand market—of any make. The Bristol tradition was not entirely lost, however, three Lodekka LD's being obtained, one of which was modified to open-top configuration. "Fok Lei" were happy also to obtain three Daimlers—two CVG6's and a CCG6. The two Leyland Titans which completed their first eight double-deckers were not the ideal choice, not because of any objection to the proven qualities of PD3's but simply because another engine type, 0.600's, encroached upon Gardner standardisation. But at the time not another suitable Gardner-engined double-decker seemed to be available anywhere in the UK! At one stage, 3-axle Guy double-deckers from Johannesburg were under consideration.

Fleet numbers of double-deck buses fell in a new series commencing at 201, with a prefix to-denote the chassis type. Yellow and cream livery was applied to all the double-deckers, of which the first four were prepared for service in Macau by "Fok Lei" themselves, while all others from 205 onwards, were prepared in Hong Kong, by Union Auto. Only the latter had the new style fleet name which was applied on both body sides above the cab windows. A little later, three additional double-deckers were purchased, two of which were Bristol KSW and one a further Leyland PD3.

The preparation of Macau's roads to make them suitable for double-deck operation necessitated the monumental

ABOVE: Landfall 1975! 418-years after the arrival of the Portuguese, in 1557, the first ever British double-deck bus is landed on Macanese soil from the barge that had brought it and three others from Hong Kong where they had been transferred from the container-ship that had brought them from England. *(John Shearman*

task of raising literally hundreds of overhead signboard, many illuminated, to prove adequate clearance. By contrast it was trees on the two islands that caused most problems although one unusual hazard was encountered on—or more correctly, above—the road leading to Taipa village where a verandah overhung the narrow carriageway so that drivers of double-deck buses required some kind of warning to remind them to steer away from danger. An accompanying

RIGHT: The route-proving cavalcade breaks new ground as the first ever double-deck buses were driven across the bridge to Taipa and causeway to Coloane. Here the veteran Bristol breakdown car leads the Daimler CC203, and Bristol Lodekka LD204. The minibus—M-18-54 about to overtake the line was the service bus of a local CTPEMI route. *(John Shearman*

LEFT: Preparations for double-deck bus operations nearly always include the pruning of overhanging branches from roadside trees and Coloane was no exception. Here Daimler CCG6, still carrying registration number 3260 NU, supplemented by local trade plates, negotiates road upgrading as well as brushing aside the leaves on its first route-proving journey to Coloane in June 1975. An unrepainted lowheight Bristol LD Lodekka, NBD 905, follows. *(John Shearman*

photograph illustrates the hazard—and the remedy—a yellow and white painted line in the road.

The first—and only—double-deck bus routes in Macau were those to Taipa and Coloane which commenced on 16th June 1975 with the three Daimlers and Lodekka LD204, being available for service. Open-top operation of LD206 was sanctioned a few weeks later. The basic service on routes, 11, 21 and 21A, did not require eleven double-deckers under normal weekday conditions but heavy weekend and holiday traffic produced such demands that additional journeys and, therefore, additional high capacity buses, were required.

As part of the Company's eventual aim of achieving one-man-operation—after allowing both public and crews to become accustomed to one-way passenger-flow with

seated conductresses—the double-deckers were, from the outset, provided with desks for seated conductresses, including the less suitable rear-entrance types. The low chassis of the Lodekkas prevented the provision of front entrances.

CV201, CV202 and (PD)211 were the only semi-automatic buses in Macau during the 'core years' that form the basis for this book.

It is believed that the demise of double-deck bus operation in Macau came to an end around 1988 when the new companies were formed. By that time the hardy survivors had worked under Macau's demanding conditions for more than twelve years. Good value for "Fok Lei's" money from relatively inexpensive, but highly durable, second-hand vehicles.

Macau fleet number	Macau regn. number	Chassis make and type	Chassis number	UK reg number	Date of Macau regn.	Year chassis built	Body layout as at Dec 1981	Principal previous UK operator
CV201	M-87-56	Daimler CVG6-30	30075	PBN 661	6.75	1960	H43/30+15FEXSD,sc	Bolton Corporation
CV202	M-87-57	Daimler CVG6-30	30078	PBN 664	6.75	1960	H43/30+15FEXSD,sc	Bolton Corporation
CC203	M-87-58	Daimler CCG6	20019	3260 NU	6.75	1963	H37/20+?FED,CXSD,sc	Chesterfield Corporation
LD204	M 87-59	Bristol LD5G	120,115	NBD 905	6.75	1956	LH33/28+10REXSD,sc	United Counties Omnibus Company
LD205	M-87-60	Bristol LD6G	108,118	SNN 77	6.75	1955	LH33/27+12REXSD,sc	Mansfield District Services
LD206	M-87-61	Bristol LD6G	100- 064	JDL 997	6.75	1954	OL33/28+10REXSD,sc	Southern Vectis Omnibus Company
PD207	M-87-62	Leyland PD3/4	573953	LCK 766	6.75	1958	H41/31+?FEXSD,sc	Ribble Motor Services
PD208	M-87-63	Leyland PD3A/1	6101 87	VHE202	6.75	1961	H41/31+?FEXSD,sc	Yorkshire Traction Company
(K)209	M-07-1 5	Bristol KSW6G	118. 032	YHT922	76/77	1957	OH38/22+10FED,RXSD,sc	Bristol Omnibus Company
(K)210	M-07-1 6	Bristol KSW6G	118. 037	YHT927	76/77	1957	H38/22+10FED,RXSD,sc	Bristol Omnibus Company
(PD)211	M-42-67	Leyland PD3A/2	1611981	UBN905	76/77	1962	H41/28+?FED,CXSD,sc	SELNEC—previously Bolton Cpn.

*(table heading above: **DOUBLE-DECK BUS FLEET FROM 1975** · *Initally Fleet Numbered xx201-211*)*

LEFT: It is often that trees present a hazard for the operators of double-deck buses over new routes. Here, in Taipa village, an overhanging verandah posed a problem. Too costly in compensation to remove, it was potentially a disaster spot should the upper-deck of a fully loaded bus strike it. The answer lay in yellow and white markings in the road, seen here in the course of being painted. This proved adequate in successfully drawing the attention of drivers to the danger. LD206 was the staff-bus in attendance. It was also used for tree pruning. *(John Shearman*

CV201 & 202—Daimler CVG6-30—*New to Bolton Corporation*

These two Daimlers were delivered direct to Macau in early 1975 and were reconditioned by "Fok Lei" in its own workshops. Originally registered PBN 661/4 in Britain, with chassis numbers 300075/8, they were allocated registration numbers M-87-56 and M-87-57 respectively on being registered in Macau on Monday 16th June 1975, on which day double-deck service was inaugurated. They were from the same batch as KMB 2D4-2D7.

These two Daimlers had the very first Gardner 6LW engines in Macau—the 6LW being the 6-cylinder equivalent of the Company's standard 5LW engine, while transmission was via the Daimatic, semi-automatic, gearbox, In fact, these two buses, together with later arrival Leyland 211, were the only semi-automatic transmission buses in Macau and were, consequently the most popular

Vehicle Specification: Daimler CVG6-30		
Chassis:	Daimler CVG6-30	
Engine:	Gardner 6LW	
Gearbox:	semi-automatic gearbox with Daimatic control	
Body make:	East Lancashire Coachbuilders	
Body layout:	H41/30FEXDS,sc	
Date introduced:	1975	Width: 8ft
Total:	2	Height: 14ft 6in
Length:	30ft	Wheelbase: 18ft 6in

with driving staff, as a result of which CV201 & 202 probably accumulated the highest mileage in the fleet.

To provide for a seated conductress—in which form all double-deckers entered Macau service—the East Lancs. body was reduced in capacity, from H41/32F to

ABOVE: The two ex-Bolton Daimler CVG6's were parked at Barra in May 1975, awaiting the commencement of double-deck operations on 16th June 1975, having been overhauled and re-painted by "Fok Lei". *(Mike Davis*

RIGHT: CV201 was seen here in service in November 1976 as it approached the bus station at the end of its journey from Taipa Island, via the bridge, on Route 11. This was previously Bolton Corporation PBN 661. *(Derek Lucas*

60

H41/30F. The front entrance/exit remained as did the sliding door, and apart from the deep sliding tropical windows, the two buses looked very much as they did when built in 1960. Despite their larger size, these two CVG6's were never converted to dual doorway and centre staircase as was the shorter CC203.

As with all Macau-painted buses, no fleetname appeared but fleet numbers were applied. CV202 later became the first Macau bus to carry over-all advertising—reportedly for Tsing Tao beer but other advertisements followed.

CV201/2 were new in 1960 and withdrawn by SELNEC (who absorbed the Bolton fleet on formation of the PTE) on expiry of the second, five-year certificate of fitness and were, some time later, bought by Rennies—in June 1973—but immediately prior to being sold to Macau by Sykes, the Barnsley dealer, both CV201 and 202 had spent some months in the fleet of Rennies of Dunfermline.

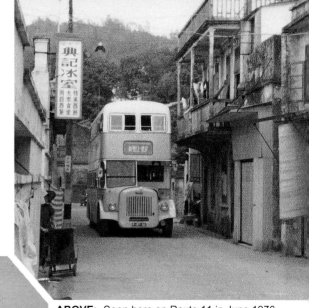

ABOVE: Seen here on Route 11 in June 1976, CV201 negotiates the narrow street past the overhanging verandah at the approach to Taipa village, seen previously. Unfortunately, the shadow of the bus almost obscures the yellow and white line in the road. *(John Shearman*

LEFT: Such was the popular attraction of the two islands, even the capacity of double-deck buses was pressed to the limit and scenes of attempted overcrowding such as this became an operating nightmare. *(John Shearman*

BELOW: By 1981, the popularity of the double-deckers continued and CV202 had a full load when seen at midday on a December day that year. The livery had been simplified to half-and-half, cream over yellow, by this time—see front cover. *(Mike Davis*

CC203—Daimler CCG6—New to Chesterfield Corporation

This bus, which was numbered CC203 by "Fok Lei" and was also reconditioned and prepared for service in the workshops near the Barra terminus. CC203 was initially operated by Chesterfield Corporation and came from the same batch as Kowloon's 2Dl-3. The registration of CC203 in Derbyshire was 3260 NU, while the chassis number was 20019. It was the newest of Macau's double-deck buses, having been built in 1963.

The Daimler CCG6 chassis had a constant mesh gearbox and never became popular, so this 27 ft long version was a somewhat rare bird, the majority of Daimlers having either pre-selective, or latterly, semi-automatic gearboxes, and were classified as CVG, whereas the second 'C' in 'CCG' indicates the constant mesh gearbox. As was the case with the other two Daimlers, the CVG6's, the engine was the Gardner 6LW.

The Weymann 'Orion' body was fitted with deep sliding tropical windows prior to entering service. For operation with a seated conductress, the lower deck capacity was reduced by two, to H37/26 FEXS, D (sc), the power operated folding doors being retained. Allocated Macau registration number M-87-58, CC203 entered service on 17th June 1975, the second day of double-deck operation.

During 1977 CC203 was rebuilt with centre stairs to become H37/20+15FED,CXSD (sc)—with both front and centre doorways *single* width.

After leaving Chesterfield, CC203 had passed to John Shennan of Drogan-by-Ayr before being exported.

Vehicle Specification: Daimler CCG6	
Chassis:	Daimler CCG6LW
Engine:	Gardner 6LW
Gearbox:	Four-speed manual gearbox and conventional clutch
Body make:	Weymann
Body layout:	H37/28FEXSD(sc) later H37/20+15FED,CXSD(sc)
Date introduced:	1975
Total:	1
Length:	27ft
Width:	7ft 11in
Height:	14ft 7in
Wheelbase:	16ft 4in

ABOVE: CC203, formerly Chesterfield Corporation 3260 NU, seen here in April 1975, prior to entry into service and before the fitting of tropical windows. (Mike Davis

LEFT: The same vehicle shortly after entering service working on route 21 between Macau and Coloane, via Taipa. It still had its original double-width forward entrance/exit and staircase at this point. (E. L. Rees

ABOVE: The limitations imposed by a single doorway for both entry and exit in a busy operating environment soon became apparent and CC203 was extensively rebuilt. The new arrangement included a centre staircase and two single-width passenger doorways; forward entrance and centre exit with a seated conductress. This November 1977 view shows the high quality of the conversion. *(David Withers*

LEFT: This third off-side view of CC203 serves to show the repositioned staircase while retaining only three opening upper-deck side windows. Compare this with the efforts made to increase the number of opening on the later buses in the double-deck fleet. *(David Withers*

LD204—Bristol Lodekka LD5G
New to United Counties Omnibus Co Ltd

LD204 was the last of the first four double-deck buses to be completely reconditioned by "Fok Lei" in Macau and had been registered NBD 902 when in the UK with United Counties and M-87-59 in Macau. Built in 1956, it had chassis number 120.115. LD204 was a fairly standard Bristol/ECW Lodekka and was the only Gardner 5LW powered double-decker to be bought by "Fok Lei". It seems that this was sufficiently powerful to cope with the stiff climb to the top of the bridge to Taipa Island.

This bus was not operated by any other firm in the UK other than UCOC.

Vehicle Specification: Bristol LD5G	
Chassis:	Bristol Lodekka LD5G
Engine:	Gardner 5LW
Gearbox:	Five-speed manual gearbox.
Body make:	Eastern Coachworks
Body layout:	LH33/26REXS,G(sc)
Date introduced:	1975
Total:	1
Length:	27ft
Width:	8ft
Height:	13ft 4in
Wheelbase:	16ft 8½in

were commenced, initially being used largely on the 21 to Coloane.

As was the case with all three Lodekkas, LD204 was unsuitable for front-entrance–rear-exit–passenger-flow because the low chassis frame, inherent in the type, prohibited the addition of a front entrance.

LEFT: Numerically the first of the three "Fok Lei" Bristol Lodekkas, LD204 was on layover, between duties when this November 1976 photograph was taken. The sloping upper margin to the cab door and window and the cab door has a horizontal lower edge, both of which features identify this body as a later ECW Lodekka 'Mk2' style. *(Martin Weyell*

BELOW: A nearside view showing the sloping valance which corresponds to the similar outline of the cab windows. *(E. L. Rees*

The ECW body was of the second style, known within ECW as a 'Mk2', introduced in 1956 (DOGGETT & TOWNSIN 1993) and featuring a sloping valance to the underside of the canopy and corresponding top edge to the cab side windows. The lower border of the window in the driver's door was also horizontal, as opposed to curved—compare with LD205, a year older, opposite.

The body of this bus was originally fitted with manual, conductor-operated, rear, platform doors but, prior to entry into Macau Service, a sliding gate was fitted, to be controlled by the seated conductress. One lower deck seat was removed and the layout became LH33/26REXS,G(sc).

LD204 was, with CV201/2, placed into service in Macau on 16th June 1975, the day on which cross-bridge services

LD205—Bristol Lodekka LD6G
ex-Mansfield District and West Riding Automobile

This was another standard Bristol/ECW Lodekka, but with the more powerful Gardner 6LW engine and had chassis number 108.118. The British registration number of this 1955 bus was SNN 77 and in Macau it became M-87-60 and was fleet numbered LD205, entering service on 6th September 1975.

The ECW body was of the so-called 'Mark 1' type with a horizontal profile to the canopy valance and upper cab windows. The window in the driver's cab door also differed on LD205—and LD 206—in having a curve downwards and rearwards, producing a 'hump' effect to the cab-side.

LD205 was the first of four buses from the initial eight double-deckers to be re-conditioned in Hong Kong, by Union Auto Body Builders, and carried in full the new fleet names, applied by a sign-writer (not transfers) and fleet numbers.

In Macau the body was reseated to accommodate a seated conductress, giving a revised layout of

Vehicle Specification: Bristol LD6G		
Chassis: Bristol Lodekka LD6G		
Engine: Gardner 6LW		
Gearbox: Five-speed manual gearbox.		
Body make: Eastern Coach Works	Length:	27ft
Body layout: LH33/26REXS,D(sc)	Width:	8ft
Introduced: 1975	Height:	13ft 4in
Total: 1	Wheelbase:	16ft 8½in

LH33/26REXS,D(sc). The power operated rear platform doors were retained.

After sale by West Riding Automobile LD205 passed for a short time to John Smith of Amble, Morpeth.

RIGHT: LD205 was formerly Mansfield District SNN 77, and when seen here parked at Barra in May 1975. It remained registered M-87-60 in Macau, although it already carried its fleet number. This bus had been reconditioned and painted by UABB in Hong Kong and thus carried the hand-painted fleetname and logo. The route number screen, although retained was never again put to use. *(Mike Davis*

LEFT: By June 1983, the livery had been simplified on LD205 and all other double-deckers, to half-and-half cream over yellow, divided with a thin blue beading band. This view at Estacao Central shows the 'curved' cab side windows. The canopy valance and top edge of the offside cab windows were horizontal on earlier 'Mk2' Lodekka bodies. 'Reservado' in Portuguese on the blind equates to 'Private' in English. *(Mike Davis*

LD206—Bristol Lodekka LD6G—*New to Southern Vectis*

When operating on the Isle of Wight, this Lodekka had carried registration number JDL 997, but it later carried Macau number M-87-61—the chassis number was 100.064.

Basically a standard Bristol/ECW Lodekka, LD6G, JDL 997 had a 'Mark 1' style body—see description for LD205—and was old enough to have the long-style radiator grille of earlier Lodekkas.

Contrary to some reports, JDL 997 did not operate as an open-top bus in the UK, its roof being removed by Norths the dealer prior to shipping; the work being completed by, UABB,

Vehicle Specification: Bristol LD6G	
Chassis:	Bristol Lodekka LD6G
Engine:	Gardner 6LW
Gearbox:	Five-speed manual gearbox.
Body make:	Eastern Coach Works
Body layout:	OT33/27REXSD,sc
Date introduced:	1975
Total:	1
Length:	27ft
Width:	8ft
Height:	approximately 12ft 9in over upper deck windscreen
Wheelbase:	16ft 8¹/2in
Unladen weight:	7500kgs

RIGHT: JDL 997 at Kwai Chung container terminal, where it had just been unloaded from the ship that carried it from the Europe. The removal of the roof and part of the pillars had been undertaken by the exporting dealer Seen here, together with SNN 77, from Mansfield District Services, later to become LD205 with "Fok Lei". *(John Shearman*

BELOW: After completion of the body conversion and reconditioning, on Sunday 25th May 1975, LD206 was taken on a private tour of Hong Kong Island and was standing alongside China Motor Bus Guy Arab, M30, next to the CMB No 7 bus stand in Central Terminal. The tour ended at the Wanchai Cargo Handling Bay where LD206 was loaded onto a barge, together with LD205, PD207 and PD208 for final delivery to Macau. *(Mike Davis*

forced seats were fitted to the upper-deck, utilising the original frames. Inside, the original well-worn moquette survived.

LD206 was the first open-top double-decker to run in Macau, and by virtue of an extended private tour during the course of delivery, from Kwai Chung to the lighter at Wanchai, which involved a three-hour drive right round Hong Kong Island—reached by way of Kowloon and a trip through the Cross-Harbour Tunnel and including a visit to the Peak—it was also the first passenger-carrying open-top bus to run on Hong Kong roads—albeit not on a public service.

After LD206's arrival and entry into service, Macau led the Far East in having the first public open-top bus service; four years before City Buses introduced the ex-Bournemouth Fleetlines in Hong Kong and Matorco cut the roof off one of its Daimler CVG5's in Manila, Philippines.

During 1985, LD206 was extensively rebuilt and emerged from works with a new upper-deck windscreen and guard rails which extended the back of the upper-deck. At his time the vehicle carried 'legal lettering' to show a capacity of 71 passengers.

the Hong Kong body contractor. When removing the roof, Norths had been asked to also remove and keep intact the upper-deck front and first side-windows as a unit which was subsequently shipped inside the bus— this reduced the cubic volume of the bus, so reducing shipping charges.

Upon arrival in Hong Kong, it went straight to the Kwai Chung premises of UABB, where it was reconditioned and had the conversion to open-top completed, including the grafting back of the front window frames, which included the opening hopper-vents for added ventilation! The extra sloping windows were added by Union. (see photograph).

Laid out as LH33/27REX, LD206 originally had an open platform but UABB added a single width conductor-operated folding door. Moulded glass-fibre rein-

The fate of LD206 remains unclear but it is probable that it did not survive the 1988 reorganization of Macau's bus services.

PD207—*Leyland Titan PD3/4*—New to Ribble Motor Services

"Fok Lei" PD207 was new in 1958 as Ribble number 1603 (LCK 766) and had chassis number 573953. This bus was similar to the Titan PD3/4's numberd PD18/19 and T4-7 in the fleet of Hong Kong's China Motor Bus Co. All were in the KCK and LCK registered batches delivered to Ribble in 1958.

Prior to being purchased by "Fok Lei", PD207 had spent some time in the fleet of Ensign, Hornsey.

Like LD205/6 and PD208, PD207 was reconditioned at Kwai Chung, by UABB, prior to onward shipment across the Pearl River estuary to Macau in mid-May 1975. It was then parked out of use for some months before being converted to half-cab layout prior to entering service in the latter half of 1976, more than a year after arriving in Macau. When eventually registered, PD207 received the number M-87-62, although this had, like those of all the original eight, been reserved with the registration authorities shortly before the commencement of double-deck operations in June 1975.

The Leyland chassis was not a first choice for "Fok Lei" as the Leyland 0.600 engine spoiled the Company's standardization on Gardner engine types. In Hong Kong, Leyland engines had been found less satisfactory than Gardners as they were faster running and tended to overheat in the hot humid summer months. Macau, however, is, except for the bridge, flatter than Hong Kong and there was less expectation of the overheating problems experienced by CMB and KMB.

The Burlingham body (number 6653) remained FH41/31FEXS, SD(sc) in Macau and when the body was altered to half-cab, the sliding passenger door was retained and no attempt was made to convert the body to centre staircase or centre doorway as was done on the ex-Bolton (PD)211 (M-42-67). A side destination screen was added in the first side window behind the door.

Vehicle Specification: Leyland PD3/4

Chassis:	Leyland Titan PD3/4
Engine:	Leyland 0.600
Gearbox:	Leyland 4--speed manual gearbox.
Body make:	Burlingham
Body layout:	H41/31FEX,SD,sc—(SD: Sliding Door)
Date built:	1958
Date introduced: 1975	Width: 8ft
Total: 1	Height: 14ft 6in
Length: 30ft	Wheelbase: 18ft 6in

ABOVE RIGHT: Before it entered service more than a year after its arrival in Macau, PD207 was converted to half-cab and a side destination blind box was fitted in the first lower-deck nearside window, immediately behind the doorway. When photographed here in November 1976, it was parked at Barra after working the 11 between Macau and Taipa. *(Martin Weyell*

RIGHT: PD207 was parked out of use and unregistered at Barra Terminus when seen here in May 1975, a year before its conversion to half-cab and subsequent entry to service *(Mike Davis*

PD208—Leyland Titan PD3A/1—New to Yorkshire Traction

Once No 707 in the Yorkshire Traction fleet with whom it was registered VHE202, PD208 carried Leyland chassis number 610178, indicating that it was built in 1961. Mechanically it was identical to the ex-Ribble PD207, a PD3/4 model—the difference being the 'St. Helens' style moulded bonnet and grille of the half-cab PD3A/1.

PD208 was another Macau bus with relatives nearby in Hong Kong. It came from the same batch of Yorkshire Traction Titan PD3A/1's as China Motor Bus training buses Tl-3.

Although PD208 was reconditioned in Hong Kong by UABB, it had been shipped to Macau prior to the arrival of the three buses for CMB. Both "Fok Lei's" PD208 and CMB's Tl-3 came to their new owners via Ensign, Hornsey, who had acquired them between August and November 1973.

PD208 entered the service of "Fok Lei" with a body layout of H41/31FEXS,SD,sc, the Northern Counties body having lost two lower-deck seats to accommodate the seated conductress. As with PD207, the sliding passenger door was retained. PD208 was registered in Macau as M-87-63, but did not enter service until early March 1976, due to delays during overhaul.

During its Macau service, few major alterations were made except for a replacement for the moulded front and grille which can be best appreciated by reference to the accompanying illustrations. A colour photograph of PD208 appears on the back cover of this book.

Vehicle Specification: Leyland PD3A/1		
Chassis: Leyland Titan PD3A/1		
Engine: Leyland 0.600		
Gearbox: Leyland 4-speed, constant-mesh, manual		
Body make: Northern Counties		
Body layout: H41/31FEXS,SD,sc		
Date built: 1961		
Introduced: 1975		Width: 8ft
Total: 1		Height: 14ft 6in
Length: 30ft		Wheelbase: 18ft 6in

ABOVE: This view of PD208 was taken whilst it was still in largely original condition, probably in the summer of 1976, at the Taipa Village terminus of Route 11. *(John Shearman*

BELOW: By December 1981, PD208 had received a replacement grille but retained the original headlight surrounds and frontal moulding. *(John Shearman*

BELOW RIGHT: another year on say the same bus with a front of the type then being fitted to the Bristol L5G fleet, although the nearside bonnet contour was retained. *(John Shearman*

209 and 210—Bristol KSW6G—New to Bristol Omnibus Company

The Bristol KSW was the 27ft long by 8 ft wide version of the original 26ft by 7 ft 6 in Model K. That in turn was the double-deck equivalent of the Model L single-deck chassis of which "Fok Lei" had 30 in stock.

Because "Fok Lei" had a long tradition of buying Bristol chassis in second-hand form, it came as no surprise to learn of the purchase of this pair of Bristol KSW6G double-deckers. In fact, had more been available, then the Lodekkas and Leylands would probably not have been purchased.

These two double-deckers were bought in 1976 following the immediate popularity of the first eight double-deck buses placed in service in the summers of 1975 and 1976, although the original eventual aim had been for twelve double-deckers.

On arrival in Hong Kong and before being forwarded to Macau, both 209 and 210 were sent to UABB at Kwai Chung, Hong Kong, where they were converted to have dual doorways—a new entrance being fitted at the front of the lower-deck—prior to their final journey to Macau. Together with 211 (qv), a Leyland Titan, 209 and 210 carried no type-letters to their fleet numbers although it had been the original intention to use the prefix 'K'.

209—M-07-15. This bus was converted to open-top, in a similar manner to the Lodekka LD206, having been built in 1957 with chassis number 118.032. It was formerly

Vehicle Specification: Bristol KSW6G	
Chassis:	Bristol KSW6G
Engine:	Gardner 6LW
Gearbox:	Five-speed manual gearbox.
Body make:	ECW
Body layout:	209—OH38/22+10FeD,REXSD,sc
	210—H38/22+10FeD,REXSD,sc
Date built: 1957	Length: 27ft
Date introduced: 1975	Width: 8ft
Total: 2	Height (210): 14ft 6in

Bristol's number C8426 (YHT 922) and a sister to number 210—see below. 209 entered service in 1977 as M-07-15.

The original 60-seat highbridge bodywork was built by ECW with open rear platform but was altered to OH33/22FED,RXSD,sc for "Fok Lei". The roof and upper-deck window pillars were removed in the same manner as on LD206 prior to the despatch of the bus from Norths in the UK to "Fok Lei". Some time later, an offside emergency door was provided in the lower saloon, as on LD206, and the capacity increased to OH38/22+10.

During 1985/6, 209 was again extensively rebuilt, including the replacement of certain pillars and other body framing. At the same time, a Daimler semi-automatic gearbox was installed.

BELOW: "Fok Lei's" second open top bus, No 209, was largely unaltered from the condition in which it entered Macau service when photographed circa 1978, retaining the original livery and inscriptions on the upper-deck side panels. *(Ian Lynas*

71

210—M-07-16. This bus was also rebuilt during its reconditioning in Hong Kong, but it retained the covered top highbridge ECW bodywork, although altered, like 209, to a front entrance and rear exit layout with a seated conductress. Part of the conversion by UABB included the fitting of an additional window pillar in the last—radiused—side windows on the upper-deck each side, in a manner similar to that used by CMB on its Southdown Leyland PD3's, thus allowing for an additional deep opening window. An unusual enlarged bonnet housing replaced the original and this is supposed to have been to improve the circulation of air around the engine compartment.

Formerly C8431 (YHT 927) in the Bristol fleet, the chassis number was 118.037, the very last K type built. The bodywork became H33/22FE, RXS, D(sc).

210 entered service late in 1976 as M-07-16. Lei" had

ABOVE: "Fok Lei" Bristol KSW6G, No 210, standing at the Taipa Village terminus of Route 11 shortly after entering service. It had originally been painted by UABB to include the company logo-come-fleet-name, as applied to all other buses painted by them. After its brief moment of film fame in Kowloon livery, 210 was returned to yellow and cream but minus the fleetnames. *(David Withers*

RIGHT: Nos 210 and 211, see page 74, at the Kwai Chung premises of UABB with work partly completed. This photograph is included to illustrate the additional window incorporated at the rear of the upper-deck each side on both these buses. This allowed a full-depth sliding window which helped air circulation at the back of the upper-deck. *(John Shearman*

'Romance on the Bus'

210 was used in a film entitled 'Romance on the Bus' made by 'The Great Wall Movie Enterprises Ltd.' in which it was painted red to represent a Kowloon Motor Bus vehicle, although the film was made in Macau. Shortly after delivery to Macau in yellow it was repainted red for the movie and then repainted yellow again before entering service.

LEFT: For its part in a motion picture made in Macau but set in Kowloon, "Fok Lei" allowed its Bristol, No 210, to be painted red in a style similar to that of Kowloon Motor Bus. Here it poses on 16th August 1977 with the rear route number blind set for the 6—the only time that it was used for that purpose in Macau! The additional upper deck side window can be seen in this view, taken at the new *Ilha Verde* depot of "Fok Lei". *(John Shearman*

BELOW: By 1981, No 210 had been repainted into the simplified half-and-half, cream over yellow livery. Here it makes a left turn under the midday sun early in 1983. The wide, originally four track, Bristol Omnibuses route number indicator screen was utilised as a destination indicator of modest proportions. From photographic evidence, 210 seems to have spent much of its successful working life on Route 11, shuttling between Macau and Taipa Island, via the first bridge. *(Mike Davis*

211—Leyland Titan PD3A/2—New to Bolton Corporation

Another PD3 was obtained in 1976, at the same time as the two Bristol KSW's. This bus was sent as an unsolicited speculative approach by dealer Ensign, then of Grays, Essex. It came from SELNEC PTE in the form of East Lancs bodied 6672 (UBN 905), a PD3A/2 with chassis number 611981 and a full fronted cab, built around a standard St. Helens bonnet. It was new in 1962.

211 passed through Hong Kong, where it was reconditioned by the same firm—Union Auto Body Builders (UABB)—that reconditioned Nos 205-210, prior to onward shipment to Macau. The body was essentially similar to those of "Fok Lei's" two Daimler CVG6's and featured a forward doorway and staircase and had a sliding door. It had been the intention to prefix the fleet number 'PD' as with the others of the type in the fleet.

Alterations undertaken by UABB included the removal of the staircase to the centre position, the provision of a single-width centre exit with folding door, the reduction of the front entrance to single-width and modification of the front sliding door so that it only opened part-way to match the reduced front doorway. A desk for the seated conductress was fitted between the two doorways.

Other, less dramatic, alterations completed by UABB included the provision of two additional upper-deck side

Vehicle Specification: Leyland PD3A/2	
Chassis:	Leyland Titan PD3A/2
Engine:	Leyland 0.600
Gearbox:	Four-speed pneumpcyclic gearbox.
Body make:	East Lancs
Body layout:	H41/28FE, CXS. D(sc).
Date new:	1962
Date introduced:	1975
Total:	1
Length:	30ft
Width:	8ft
Height:	14ft 6in
Wheelbase:	18ft 6in

windows each side by 'squaring-off' the front and rear window-frames, by fitting a new pillar to separate the main window area from the 'curved' portion adjacent to the respective body corner. The main area was then provided with a full-depth sliding window unit and the 'curved' residual portion was fitted with a small section of fixed glazing.

As a result of the modifications, the body layout was altered to H41/28FED,CXSD(sc). The full front was reduced to half-cab by "Fok Lei" in Macau prior to its entry into service. At an unconfirmed date, however, the front sliding doorway was replaced by a folding unit.

BELOW: "Fok Lei" No 211 was an East lancs bodied Leyland Titan PD3A/2, new to Bolton and had similar bodywork to the two Daimler CVG6's, CV201 & CV202, from the same operator. Upon its arrival in Macau, it retained its full-width driving cab buthad been altered to have a centre exit door and staircase, retaining the sliding door to the front entrance. It was photographed here near Barra, unregistered and awaiting its entry into service. *(Derek Lucas*

The bus was powered by a Leyland 0.600 engine, and unlike "Fok Lei's" other Titans, had a Leyland, pneumocyclic, semi-automatic, gearbox which—with CV201 and CV202—made it very popular with the drivers, accustomed, as they were, to heavy Bristol manual clutches and crash gearboxes.

The Macau registration number of this bus became M-42-67 and entered service late 1977 or early 1978.

ABOVE: No 211 was in its later livery, complete with advertising for Chinese Batteries when seen here leaving Coloane, at the start of its journey to Taipa and Macau. The location of the centre staircase can be seen clearly in this view, as can the small upper-deck first and last side windows that enabled the installation of additional fully opening window units. *(Ian Lynas*

LEFT: Unfortunately, a good nearside view of No 211 was not available to show the altered doorway arrangements with folding doors at both doorways. Here 211 stands in the depot next to Bristol Lodekka, LD204, although by this time both buses had lost their fleet numbers which, by this time, had been dropped by the operator. *(Mike Davis*

Double-deck Postscript

The double-deck buses served Macau for up to 13 years and carried many thousands of passengers to and fro between Macau peninsula and the islands of Coloane and Taipa.

Unfortunately, plans to extend the use of double-deckers to city services was to fall by the wayside. The sheer effort to create headroom in streets festooned with traditional Chinese-style overhead signs caused the will to erode, just at a time when relatively inexpensive buses became available from Japanese manufacturers who had improved the robustness of their products to equal that of the better British 'lightweight' chassis.

There were, however, three double-deckers that could be said to feature on the fringes of our story. The first two of these were said to have been ordered by "Fok Lei", through TSW(HK)Ltd, and took the form of two ex-London Transport 'DMS' type Fleetlines (DMS2207 and DMS2218—OJD 207R and OJD 218R). Both vehicles were refurbished by Ensignbus, of Purfleet, Essex, who also repainted them into "Fok Lei's" yellow and cream livery with blue lining. Unfortunately, after they had arrived in Hong Kong for transhipment to Macau, the order was cancelled and the two buses lay idle on the premises of Citybus Limited, Hong Kong, before eventually being taken into their stock and allocated the fleet numbers 44 and 45.

The third double-decker with Macau connections was a bus owned by Argos Bus Service, also of Hong Kong, which was fitted-out as a mobile 'Macau Visitors' Service Centre'. It was displayed at various sites around Hong Kong but never visited Macau. It was fitted with domestic-type air-conditioning units for which an external electricity supply was required. This bus was another Fleetline, this time from the South Yorkshire PTE. fleet, where it had been registered OET103M.

ABOVE: OJD 218R was one of a pair of former London Transport 'DMS' Fleetlines destined for Macau but which never actually progressed any further than Hong Kong. It was in Macau livery, at the Hung Hom, (Hong Kong) premises of Citybus when photographed in 1983. They eventually became part of the Citybus, Hong Kong, fleet in 1985/6. This particular example ended its days with Argos Bus Service, also of Hong Kong; the other went to Guangzhou. *(John Shearman*

LEFT: Once OET 103M in the fleet of South Yorkshire Passenger Transport Executive, this Fleetline was the property of Argos Bus Service, Hong Kong, but was not used as a bus during its time, from 1985, as the Macau Visitors' Service Centre. It carried a domestic-style air-conditioner in an off-side upper-deck rear window. This bus was never intended to visit Macau and returned to bus service with Argos a few years later.
(John Shearman

The non-British Vehicles—Isuzu single-deck buses

Following the purchase of the Albion Vikings, buses in Macau were, for a number of years, to be largely non-British in origin but, to complete the picture, these *are* included.

1983-type: During 1983, "Fok Lei" introduced four Isuzu single-deck bus chassis which were delivered via the Hong Kong body maker Wong Ming, who fitted 38-seat, airconditioned, bodies suitable for driver-only-operation, using Bell Punch 'Autofare' Fareboxes . These enabled "Fok Lei" to upgrade the 3A bus service, used by foreign tourists, which ran between the Hong Kong–Macau hydrofoil and Jetfoil piers and the City centre.

The chassis featured a set-back front-axle and front engine which was alongside the driver in a similar manner to the Leyland Vikings delivered late in 1981. These four buses represent the first Japanese chassis for full size bus operation to be ordered by "Fok Lei" and also represented change in being of lightweight specification.

The Wong Ming bodywork was somewhat similar to that supplied to the Macau 'Islands' company on Bedford

Vehicle Specification: Isuzu—1983 & 1984	
Chassis:	Isuzu
Engine:	Isuzu
Gearbox:	Five-speed synchromesh with friction clutch
Body make:	1983-type Wong Ming, Hong Kong
	1984-type Sun Cheong, Hong Kong
Body layout:	1983—B38F,DOO,a/c; or 1984 B40FED,RXD
Total:	1982: 4; 1984: 6

SB chassis except that the entrance was ahead of the front wheels and the window frames and body pillars were vertical. No use was made of three by two seating in view of the tourist traffic envisaged but, for the first time, the staff accepted driver-only-operation on full sized buses and were fitted.

1984 -type: A further six Isusus were delivered in 1984 and these differed from the previous examples in having 40-seat bodies by Sun Cheong, similar to those on the rebodied Bristols and the new Vikings delivered in 1981, again they had a front entrance and centre exit.

Intrestingly, the registration numbers allocated werte re-issued in the M-44-xx series.

ISUZU–fleet list

WONG MING BODIES—B40FEX, OMO

Regn number	Chassis number	Date introduced
MB-20-94	?	1983
MB-20-95	?	1983
MB-20-96	?	1983
MB-20-97	?	1983

SUN CHEONG BODIES B38D

M-44-19	?	1984
M-44-27	?	1984
M-44-43	?	1984
M-44-54	?	1984
M-44-58	?	1984

ABOVE: One of the four airconditioned Isuzus introduced for use on Route 3A linking the Jetfoil terminat to the central area. *(Mike Davis*

RIGHT: The 1983/84 Isuzus were non-airconditioned and looked very similar to the 1981 Albions. *(Roger Bailey*

Nissan Civilian—large minibuses

In order to bring a regular bus service to many narrower side streets, "Fok Lei" purchased and placed in service a small fleet of what could be described as 'large minibuses' based on the Nissan Civilian which is factory mass-produced and a big-brother to the Nissan Echo 14-seat minibus once so popular as Public Light Buses in Hong Kong. With seats for 25 the Civilian is powered by the Nissan 2200cc diesel, also used in the 'Echo' and many Hong Kong taxis. A product of Nissan Motors Ltd—as opposed to Nissan Diesel Ltd—it owes more to the car industry in concept than to the traditional bus, thus it is not referred to here as a 'midi', which would liken it to the Albion Nimbus and similar types. By the end of 1981 "Fok Lei" had in service 12 Civilians although one contemporary report claimed that four more were on order.

During the 1980's, these minibuses operated on four routes, 6. 7. 8 & 9, and ran to a similar traffic pattern as the conventional buses. They could be likened to the Hong Kong 'green' minibuses (Maxi-cabs), running on set routes and charging set flat fares - a flat 70¢ in 1981.

Vehicle Specification: Nissan Civilian

Chassis:	Nissan Civilian
Engine:	Nissan
Gearbox:	Five-speed synchromesh
Body make:	Nissan Civilian
Body layout:	M25
Date introduced:	1979
Total:	12

Unlike the bus fleet, the minibuses carried the Company name in Portuguese along the bodyside, together with the initials 'CAFL'—earlier examples also carried the 'logo' first applied to the 1975 Albion Vikings—the name on a white oval divided between the three languages by long blue arrows.

These vehicles are believed to have been amongst the first buses in the fleet to carry MA registration numbers.

Nissan Civilian fleet list

NISSAN STEEL BODIES—B25C

Regn. numbers	Year introduced
MA-24-97	1979
MA-32-43	1979
MA-32-44	1979
MA-32-45	1979
MA-32-46	1979
MA-32-47	1979
MA-32-48	1979
MA-32-49	1979
MA-32-50	1979
MA-34-07	1979
MA-48-24	1979
MA-48-25	1979

LEFT: Nissan Civilian MA-32-44 typifies the type in this December 1981 view taken near the Lisboa Hotel at the foot of the Macau—Taipa bridge. The Company's initials 'CAFL' only appeared on these 'large minibuses'. *(Mike Davis*

LEFT: This offside rear view of a Civilian shows more clearly the full company name in Portuguese, under the side windows. MA-32-44 was turning left outside the Post Office building. *(Mike Davis*

The Buses of Companhia de Auto-Omnibus de Taipa

Auto-Omnibus de Taipa ran the local bus service on Taipa Island until it was reformed, together with the Coloane operator, into CTPEMI, in September 1974.

In addition to the two Austins acquired from "Fok Lei", described below, the Taipa bus operator ran three buses with crude, locally built, bodywork. The vehicles run between January 1973 and September 1974 were:

Commer

Commer—M-10-41—was a forward-control model, fitted with a very substantial full-fronted, timber-built body with seats for about 30 people. It is believed that it was new in the early 1950's. It had curved perspex windows in the front corners, either side of the windscreen. An additional door was built into the back of the body. During the period 1973-74, it was idle for long periods but was in use at some busy times when it was photographed.

Thames

These two similar vehicles had normal-control Thames chassis, dating from about the early 1950's, and local, timber-built, bodywork similar to that of the Commer, M-10-41, except that they were normal control vehicles and only sat about 25. An additional door was provided in the back of both bodies. Little else is known of these vehicles. Both were largely out of use in both January 1973 and July 1974 but did see occasional use.

Austin

These two identical Austin buses—M-13-61 & M-25-50—were obtained second-hand from "Fok Lei" and apart from a change of fleet name, remained as already described except that their livery was the dark green of the Taipa company. They were fitted with the "Fok Lei" interpretation of a pre-war ECW body and had two door-ways, retaining the swing gates fitted by "Fok Lei".

LEFT: This June 1972 offside view of the Commer M-10-41—operated by Auto-Omnibus de Taipa shows the overall appearance of the vehicle with its locally fabricated timber body, with curved perspex corner windows at the front. *(Peter Miller*

BELOW: It is not possible to identify which of the two almost identical Ford Thames buses this is. It was photographed in June 1972 under brilliant sunshine. *(E. L. Rees*

ABOVE: The Austins acquired from "Fok Lei" has 33-seat bodies with swing gates as standard on its former owner's vehicles. M-13-61 is seen here loading at Taipa Ferry Pier in June 1972. (E. L. Rees

Auto-Omnibus de Taipa   *Fleet list — 1973-74*

Reg. number	Chassis make	Chassis number	Notes
M-13-61	Austin	214140	Engine number: 51JU/1188
M-25-50	Austin	?	
M-10-41	Commer	?	
M-13-26	Ford Thames	?	
M-17-45	Ford Thames	?	

BELOW: M-25-50 the other of the pair of Austins, differed from M-13-61 only in having three horizontal bars across the radiator grille—a feature that identifies it in the photograph on page 41. (E. L. Rees

The Buses of 路環利安巴士公司
(Lo Wan Lee On—Coloane Island)
This company only publicly displayed its title in Chinese characters

Lo Wan Lee On ran the local bus service on Coloane Island until it was absorbed into CTPEMI, in September 1974.

In addition to the Morrises acquired from "Fok Lei", described below, Lo Wan Lee On ran a lorry/bus and a large minibus. Livery was red with the company name in white Chinese characters along each side. No Portuguese was used. The vehicles operating between January 1973 and August 1974 were:

Commer lorry-bus

M-13-06: This was a normal-control Commer lorry chassis dating from the late 1950's. Passenger accommodation was provided on bus-type seats inside the extended cab, and on hard bench sets in the back of the lorry, under a metal roof and protected by canvas side screens. The bodywork was very basic and definitely local.

This vehicle was used on the irregular route from Coloane Village via Hac-Sa to Ka-Ho although the odd journey was made across the causeway to Taipa during 1973/74.

Morris

Lo Wan Lee On acquired three, or all four, of the Morris buses previously operated by "Fok Lei"—M-12-18, M-12-19, M-12-56 and M-12-57. They were used on their intra-island route until the opening of the causeway between Coloane and Taipa after which they also ran on the inter-island route.

By July 1973 there were only three in evidence (M-12-57 having been converted to a lorry) of which one—M-12-19—was wheel-less and abandoned. By July 1974, M-12-19 was still derelict while M-12-56—recently refurbished—and M-12-18 were in service.

For their intra-island operation, the rear skirt panels were cut away very sharply, so sharply that the step-well of rear entrance protruded in an ungainly fashion although, in being refurbished M-12-56 had had its rear profile reinstated.

In September 1974, M-12-56 and M-12-18 remained in daily service and were transferred to CTPEMI.

Lo Wan Lee On (Coloane) Fleet list–1973-74

Reg. number	Chassis make	Chassis number	Notes
M-12-18	Morris	plate missing	
M-12-19	Morris	51771	6-cyl diesel of unknown (BMC?) make
M-12-56	Morris	plate missing	
M-13-06	Commer	?	normal control dual-purpose bus/lorry
M-18-54	Isuzu minibus	?	large minibus
M- ? - ?	Ford Transit	?	derelict by January 1973

TOP of PAGE: The Commer lorry-bus that ran on Coloane Island, seen here in 1972. *(E. L. Rees*

BELOW: Two of the Coloane Morrises with Beadle look-alike bodywork seen in July 1973 while still sporting the company name—Lo Wan Lee On—in full in Chinese. M-12-18 retained its original bright metal grille until withdrawn by CTPEMI in 1975/6. *(John Shearman*

LEFT: This view shows M-12-19 in a derelict condition in July 1973, from which it never recovered! The rear body had been cut away so sharply that the rear passenger steps were exposed the new skirt line. The close resemblance to Beadle products is extraordinary and has been the subject of much research. The only answer seems to be that they were copied from the Bedford-Beadle buses of "Fok Lei". The original concealed radiator has been exposed by the missing panel. *(John Shearman*

LEFT CENTRE: This July 1973 rear view of M-12-18, shows the cut-away rear panels, said to be necessary to negotiate the steep slope down to the causeway between Coloane and Taipa islands. This bus was later refurbished and its rear panels restored. *(John Shearman*

BELOW: The third of the Morrises with 'Beadle-look-alike' bodies, seen here in July 1973 after being refurbished and immediately prior to being absorbed into the CTPEMI fleet. Behind the Morris is the rear of the Commer lorry-bus. *(John Shearman*

Minibuses.

In 1973 an un-registered Ford Transit had been set aside to rot at the depot and nothing else is known of this vehicle.

Probably to replace the Transit, Lo Wan Lee On operated a large Isuzu minibus, M-18-54, on the route within Coloane but although it was not observed on the causeway route, it may well have taken its turn at busy times, this latterly being the preserve of the Morrises.

Neither of the minibuses was photographed whilst with Lo Wan Lee On.

The Buses of
Companhia de Transporte de Passageiros Entre Macau E Ilhas Ltda

Translated literally:- Company of Transport of Passengers between Macau and the Islands—referred to hereafter as CTPEMI

Buses inherited from the Taipa and Colone companies

As outlined on pages 10 and 11, CTPEMI was formed in September 1974 to take-over the operations of the two island bus operators and embraced the ferry operator which, with the opening of the first bridge to link the mainland with Taipa and, via the causeway, Colaone, was facing a bleak future. CTPEMI inherited a motly collection of buses, which have already been described. All buses except the Commer and Thames—but including the Commer lorry-bus— were repainted into CTPEMI buff-colour livery. The situation in May 1975 was:

Commer—ex-Auto-Carros de Taipa

When M-10-41 was seen and photographed in May 1975, the Macau equivalent of the Road Tax Disc, in the windscreen, was still current, although the bus appeared to have been out of use for some time, judging by a flat tyre and the lack of tyre tracks in the soft earth on which it stood.

Thames—ex-Auto-Carros de Taipa

Of the two buses noted on Taipa at the end of May 1975—M-13-26 and M-17-45—only the former carried any registration plates. Like M-10-41, it too was licensed.

Austin—ex-"Fok Lei" and Taipa

These two buses were described fully in the section dealing with "Fok Lei" vehicles and again under Auto-Carros de Taipa and remained essentially unchanged,

BELOW: By May 1975, Austin M-13-61 had been absorbed into the CTPEMI fleet and remained in service within the islands until replaced by a Bedford VAS. *(Mike Davis)*

CTPEMI Fleet List—1974-1981

Inherited vehicles have been described under previous headings

ALL BODIES BY WONG MING (HONG KONG)

Regn no.	Chassis make	Chassis number	Seats	Year new	Disposal
M-83-27	Bedford SB 5	DW ?	B49F	1974	to TCM
M-83-29	Bedford SB 5	DW451065	B49F	1974	to TCM L03
M-84-24	Bedford SB 5	DW453451	B52F	1975	to TCM
M-84-25	Bedford SB 5	DW ?	B52F	1975	to TCM L04
M-84-71	Bedford SB 5	DW451111	B52F	1975	to TCM L05
M-84-73	Bedford SB 5	DW451101	B52F	1975	to TCM L06
M-85-39	Bedford SB 5	DW452451	B52F	1975	to TCM
M-85-40	Bedford SB 5	DW ?	B52F	1975	to TCM
M-98-34	Daihatsu ?	?	B25F	1977	to TCM-not used
M-98-35	Daihatsu ?	?	B25F	1977	to TCM-not used
MA-11-36	Bedford VAS 5	?	B25F	c1978	to TCM L11
MA-11-37	Bedford VAS 5	?	B25F	c1978	to TCM L10
MA-61-08	Bedford SB 5	?	B52F	1980	to TCM
MA-61-09	Bedford SB 5	?	B52F	1980	to TCM L12
MA-74-01	Bedford SB 5	?	B52F	1981	to TCML 13
MA-74-02	Bedford SB 5	?	B52F	1981	to TCM L14

NB: There is no evidence to suggest that registration number swapping occurred in this fleet.

except in colour. Their "Fok Lei" copies of Eastern Coach Works bodywork had seats for 33 passengers. One at least survived in 1976. Registration numbers were M-13-6l and M-25-50.

Morris—ex-"Fok Lei" and Lo Wan Lee On

Full details of these Morris buses will be found in the "Fok Lei" section. Only two M-12-18 and M-12-56 became active members of the CTPEMI fleet and it is presumed that the third was scrapped. The body layout was FB33FEX,REX,G—just as it was when they were sold by "Fok Lei" to the former Lo Wan Lee On company. After being absorbed into CTPEMI, the Morrises ran the intra island services until replaced by new vehicles and it is very unlikely that they ever ventured across the bridge into Macau proper.

Isuzu large mini-bus— ex-Lo Wan Lee On

This vehicle, M-18-54, was inherited from Lo Wan Lee On and falls into that category unknown in Britain which is too big for a 'minibus' and of the wrong style to be a true 'midibus' and so, for want of a better description the term 'Large Mini bus' has been adopted here. It worked largely within Coloane serving the one route on that island. This 23 seat factory built vehicle was still to be seen, albeit out of passenger service, in late 1982 inside the company's compound near the Lisboa Hotel.

Bedford SB5 Buses

These eight buses were ordered for a very prompt delivery in order for them to be ready for the commencement of cross-bridge operations. The first two differed from the remaining six in a number of ways and it is believed that they were purchased as standard Hong Kong bodied products available from dealer's stock and received little modification. The subsequent six SB5's were customised to meet CTPEMI requirements. In 1980/81 a further four similar buses were added to the fleet.

The Bedford SB5 chassis was a front engined model, powered by the maker's own diesel unit driving through a 5-speed synchromesh gearbox.

Non-airconditioned—M-83-27 & M-83-29

These first two Bedford SB5's were rushed into service so quickly when the cross-bridge services commenced, in October 1974, that one at least was running in public passenger service on the local equivalent of trade plates.

The most readily identified external difference was that these first two had shallow, single-line, destination screens

Vehicle Specification—Bedford SB5	
Chassis:	Bedford NJM - SB5
Engine:	Bedford 3.3 litre diesel
Gearbox:	Bedford 5-speed, manual
Body make:	Wong Ming (Hong Kong)
Total:	12
Length:	30ft (2) or 29ft (remainder)

that fitted below the peaked front of the roof canopy.

Internally, they were not fitted with airconditioning and had 2+2 seating for 49 and a single combined front entrance/exit with power-operated doors. All the bodies were built by Wong Ming of Kwung Tong (Kowloon) and had folding doors to the front entrance/exit. Styling was more akin to a contemporary Hong Kong coach, with raked pillars and large side windows which slid full-depth to admit as much air as possible in the hot summer months. Interior fittings were of bus pattern despite outward appearances.

Both survived to pass to TCM in 1988 and lasted at least until late in 1995

RIGHT: M-83-27 was about eight months old in May 1975 when photographed outside the muddy yard on Taipa that served as a depot. This Bedford SB5 had Wong Ming bodywork, a shallow, single-line destination screen and was not airconditioned. The dark brown band below the windows and around the front was present at the time of delivery in October 1974–see page 11. *(Mike Davis*

LOWER RIGHT: M-84-24 was the first of the six 1974/75 Bedford SB's with airconditioned bodies. The larger destination screen can be compared with that in the picture above. Note the slightly different pillar spacing to accommodate the airconditioning plant amidships, behind the grille in the side panels. This photograph was taken in March 1975, prior to the addition of the dark brown band around the body, separating the lower buff colour (see back cover) from the white of the window surrounds and roof. *(Mike Davis*

Airconditioned SB5's

The other six Bedfords followed in late 1974 and early 1975 and were air-conditioned, having 3+2 seating arrangement for 52 passengers. They had an overall length of about 29ft. These air-conditioned examples had raised, single-screen destination boxes, with more room for bi-lingual place names and a route number. Their bodies, although similar to the first two, differed in minor ways. The body-pillar spacing was altered in order to accommodate the airconditioning unit within the wheelbase, its location being identified by a grille in the lower side panels.

Additional airconditioned SB's

Four additional Bedford SB's were obtained during 1980/81 and they can be identified from the earlier batch by their MA series index letters before the registration numbers. Standard Wong Ming bodywork was fitted with raked window pillars and airconditioning.

ABOVE: Airconditioned SB5, M-84-24, two months after the picture on the opposite page, following the addition of its brown band. The air-conditioned Bedfords worked the 11 between Taipa and Macau and 21/21A Coloane services. *(Mike Davis*

BELOW: Four additional Bedford SB5's were added to the CTPEMI fleet in 1980/81 and MA-61-08 was numerically the first of them. It was standing in harsh October sunshine in 1984 with no sign of air-conditioning. *(Roger Bailey*

BELOW: This line of Bedfords includes three SB5's, a partly concealed VAS5, behind M-83-27, and, to the far left, M-18-54, the illusive Isuzu large minibus. This was the CTPEMI depot on the Macau peninsula in December 1981. *(Mike Davis*

Daihatsu midi-buses

While the Bedford SB5's were ideal for the trunk cross-bridge routes, the services within the islands, particularly Coloane, required smaller vehicles. In 1977, when the inherited Isuzu large minibus required replacement, two new Diahatsu midi-buses appeared with bodywork of a similar but simplified design to that of the Bedford SB5's. They were, of course, much shorter and had ventical side window pillars. Registered M-98-34 and M-98-35, the Daihatsus had seats for 25 persons and featured a folding door behind the front wheels.

RIGHT: Daihatsu M-98-34 at Hac Sa terminus on Coloane whilst running on the one route within that island. *(Ian Lynas*

Bedford VAS

When the fleet of Morris and Austin buses required replacement, two Bedford VAS5 with approximately 35-seats were acquired for use on services within Taipa and between Taipa and Coloane. Although similar to the two Daihatsus, they were slightly bigger buses and had a layout of B35FEXD.

Vehicle Specification—Bedford VAS	
Chassis:	Bedford PJK - VAS
Engine:	Bedford 3.3 litre diesel
Gearbox:	Bedford 5-speed, manual
Body make:	Wong Ming (Hong Kong)
Body layout:	B35FEXD
Total: 2	Length: approx 26ft

LEFT: Bedford VAS5, MA-11-37 in inter island Route 1 between Hac Sa, Coloane Village and Taipa, waiting on 1st June 1983 at the Taipa Village terminus. *(Mike Davis*

Karrier—M-30-11

RIGHT: When photographed in May 1975, this bus had only just been bought by CTPEMI and still carried the name of the previous owner, a Macau factory, by whom it had been used as a staff bus. It origianally had a hinged-door, as seen here, but, by Septmeber 1975, had been fitted with the then standard 'Macau' style swing gates, 27 seats and had been repainteed in the new owners livery of sandy brown. It operated on routes within the two islands, but on one particularly busy occasion it worked across the bridge to Macau on route 21A from Coloane. *(Mike Davis*

The Buses of TRANSMAC - Transportes Urbanos de Macau, SARL
澳門新福利公共汽車有限公司—新福利—*(New Fok Lei)*

The fleet of buses previously owned by "Fok Lei" was transferred to a new organization named, in Portuguese, 'Transportes Urbanos de Macau, S.A.R.L.'—in English 'Macau Urban Transport, Ltd'. The company chooses to operate under the fleet name 'Transmac' but, perhaps more intrestingly, the Chinese characters 新福利 read 'New Fok Lei'. The livery is base white, relieved by bands of yellow and blue. The logo is a circle formed by three anti-clockwise facing blue arrows around a yellow centre and also forms the bus stop head for Transmac services. The fleet is numbered and all vehicles display a type-prefix to their number front and rear with digits below 10 being additionally prefixed by a zero: 01 to 09. The type prefix is a letter, usually the initial letter of the chassis manufacturer or the model; ie F-Fuso; R-Rosa; etc.

By 1994, the Transmac fleet consisted of over one-hundred and sixty Mitsubishi Rosa large minibuses, (fleet numbered R01-R161), a handful of Nissan Civilians, probably transferred from the former "Fok Lei" fleet (C01-C06); likewise, ten Isuzu full-sized buses (S01-S10) and thirty Mitsubishi Fuso buses F01 to F30.

In 1995, Dennis Specialist Vehicles had an order to supply ten Dennis Dart single-deck buses to Transmac, thereby rekindling the era of the British bus in Portuguese Macau. These were delivered in December 1995/January 1996 and were fleet numbered D01-D10.

The same operator has a fleet of buses in Guangzhou which carry a white livery with a red (non air-conditioned) or purple (air-cond.) band at skirt level and similar circular logo as that used by Transmac.

The Return of the British Years

The last British buses arrived in Macau circa 1981 when the final batch of Albion EVK55 Vikings entered service with "Fok Lei". The Bedford era with CTPEMI did just extend to the end of 1995 in the form of SB5's purchased as long ago as 1981 but with General Motors involvement with Isuzu, it was that maker who was to supply what had been the Bedford market in the Far East.

When, early in 1995, the title of this book was decided upon, there was no suggestion that Dennis Darts would be on the streets of Macau before this volume reached the bookshops. Perhaps, years from now, another era of British Bus Years will be recorded for posterity.

BELOW: Ten Dennis Darts on the streets of Macau bring back the influence of British bus manufacturers as providers of European quality buses with right-hand drive. Here the premier member of the D-class, D01, loads whilst working on Aeroporto Route AP1, early in 1996. There were at one time plans for Darts on the AP1 to have luggage pens and fewer seats but initially they were fully seated, in standard trim. *(Clement Lau)*

Dennis Dart

D 01 - D 10

Perhaps one of the most successful British designed and built single-deck buses of recent years has been the Dennis Dart. It has now arrived in the Far East in some numbers, appearing in Hong Kong (four operators), Singapore and Malaysia (Kuala Lumpur anf Johore Bahru). To this impressive result has recently been added Macau with ten Darts now (February 1996) operating for Transmac, SARL.

The Dennis Dart is a rear-engined model, powered by the Cummins B6 engine and fitted with an Allison fully-automatic gearbox.

The Plaxton 'Pointer' bodywork was sent out completely built-up and is arranged for maximum capacity, plated for a total of 60 passengers, including standees and fitted with sutrak airconditioning.

One proposal was to have luggage pens on buses used on AP 1 service to and from the new airport but this was not done initially.

At the time of publication, it had not been possible to

Vehicle Specification—Dennis Dart		
Fleet numbers:	D 01 to D 10	
Chassis:	Dennis Dart	
Engine:	Cummins B6	
Gearbox:	Allison fully automatic	
Body make:	Plaxton 'Pointer'	
Body layout:	B 32FED,CXD (total capacity on side of bus is 60: includes standees)	
Airconditioner:	Sutrak	
Date introduced:	December1995/January 1996	
Total:	10	Height:
Length:	9800mm nominal	Wheelbase: 5115mm
Width:	2400mm	GVW:10,500kg

link specific Dart chassis numbers to any one bus, so the story of the British bus in Macau finishes where it bagan— unable to say for certain which bus has which particular chassis!

ABOVE: On 20th January 1996, Dennis Dart D 07 was making its way towards the Jetfoil terminal, again on Route 3. *(Timothy Phillips*

BELOW: Transmac Dennis Dart No D 04 seen in service in January 1996. These buses were allocated the Route 3

linking the Jetfoil Terminal, the hotel district and the China Border—*Portas do Cerco*—and Route AP1 which provides similar links with the new *Aeroporto*. The livery adopted increases the use of yellow with only the window surrounds and roof white. *(Clement Lau*

Mitsubishi Fuso   F 01-30

To replace the collection of buses inherited from "Fok Lei", Transmac purchased thirty Mitsubishi Fuso buses with bodies by Hong Kong body builder Jit Luen These two-door buses are one man operated with driver-supervised fareboxes, as used in Hong Kong.

Clear route numbers and bilingual destinations are displayed and changed at each end of the journey.

Vehicle Specification—Mitsubishi Fuso	
Fleet numbers:	F 01-30
Chassis:	Mitsubishi Fuso BK
Engine:	Mitsubishi 6D14 175bhp
Gearbox:	Mitsubishi manual
Body make:	Jit Luen (Hong Kong)
Passenger capacity:	73, including standees
Total:	30
Length:	10.5m
GVW:	13000kgs

LEFT: Jit Luen bodied Fuso F 09 laying-over between duties at the Barra terminus of Route 5 in March 1995. Although clear destinations are displayed, the numerous via points are displayed on slip boards placed in the windscreen. *(Ron Phillips collection*

Mitsubishi Rosa   R 01-R161

For use in the narrow streets off the main roads, a fleet of standard Mitsubishi Rosa large minibuses is utilised in replacement of the life expired Nissan Civilian s inherited from "Fok Lei". These are standard reseese-steel products of the automotive industry as opposed to traditional bus coachbuilding.

Vehicle Specification—Mitsubishi Rosa		
Chassis:	Mitsubishi Rosa BE	
Engine:	Mitsubishi 103bhp diesel	
Gearbox:	Mitsubishi	
Body:	22-seat minibus	
Total:	161	
Wheelbase:	3.8m	Weight: 5500kgs

LEFT: The Transmac version of the Mitsubishi 'Rosa' 22-seat minibus in January 1996. Rosa R 24 was on the 1A to 'Jaialai' – a local shotening of the destination 'Jaialai Stadium'. Jaialai is a very popular sport in Macau and very big business. *(Clement Lau*

ABOVE: The nearside of Transmac Dennis Dart D 04, the offside of which is illustrated on page 88. The double-width front entrance and narrower centre exit doors have full-length glazing while the airconditioner 'pod' can just be seen on the roof. (*Clement Lau*

RIGHT CENTRE: Transmac Mitsubishi Rosa seen here early in 1996. (*Clement Lau*

RIGHT: Transmac Isuzu No S 08 was new to the "Fok Lei" company in the early 1980's but had been transferred to Transmac at the time of the changes to Macau's bus operators and operations. It has a 47-seat Hong Kong built bus body (*Tim Phillips*

Fuso Mitsubishi

Fleet number	Regn number
F01	MC-54-65
F02	MC-54-66
F03	MC-54-67
F04	MC-56-83
F05	MC-56-85
F06	MC-59-16
F07	MC-59-21
F08	MC-52-51
F09	MC-53-29
F10	MC-54-50
F11	MC-59-92
F12	MC-59-93
F13	MC-61-57
F14	MC-61-73
F15	MC-62-29
F16	MC-62-44
F17	MC-63-41
F18	MC-65-27
F19	MC-65-51
F20	MC-65-58
F21	MC-67-65
F22	MC-69-05
F23	MC-69-46
F24	MC-70-26
F25	MC-72-25
F26	MC-73-40
F27	MC-74-o6
F28	MC-74-11
F29	MC-74-82
F30	MC-74-79

Isuzu

Fleet number	Regn number
S01	MB-20-95
S02	MB-20-96
S03	MB-20-97
S04	MB-20-94
S05	MB-44-04
S06	M-44-19
S07	M-44-27
S08	M-44-43
S09	M-44-54
S10	M-44-58

Nissan Civilian

Fleet number	Regn numnber
C 01	MC-41-10
C 02	MC-41-11
C 03	MC-41-12
C 04	MC-41-13
C 05	MC-41-15
C 06	MC-39-59
C 07	MC-53-97

Toyota Coaster

Fleet number	Regn numnber
C 08	MF-14-85
C 09	MF-14-89
C 10	MF-14-98
C 11	MF-15-03
C 12	MF-15-04

Nissan Civilian (Staff bus)

Fleet number	Regn number
-	MA-32-14

Mitsubishi Rosa

Fleet number	Regn number
R01	MC-47-19
R02	MC-47-20
R03	MC-47_21
R04	MC-47-22
R05	MC-47-23
R06	MC-47-24
R07	MC-47-25
R08	MC-47-26
R09	MC-47-27
R10	MC-47-28
R11	MC-47-29
R12	MC-47-30
R13	MC-47-31
R14	MC-47-32
R15	MC-47-33
R16	MC-47-91
R17	MC-47-92
R18	MC-47-93
R19	MC-47-94
R20	MC-47-95
R21	MC-47-96
R22	MC-47-97
R23	MC-47-98
R24	MC-47-99
R25	MC-48-00
R26	MC-48-01
R27	MC-48-02
R28	MC-48-03
R29	MC-48-04
R30	MC-48-05
R31	MC-49-39
R32	MC-49-40
R33	MC-49-41
R34	MC-49-42
R35	MC-49-43
R36	MC-49-44
R37	MC-49-45
R38	MC-49-46
R39	MC-49-47
R40	MC-50-03
R41	MC-50-04
R42	MC-50-06
R43	MC-50-07
R44	MC-50-08
R45	MC-50-09
R46	MC-67-51
R47	MC-67-60
R48	MC-67-63
R49	MC-67-70
R50	MC-67-73
R51	MC-65-48
R52	MC-65-50
R53	MC-65-53
R54	MC-65-59
R55	MC-65-53
R56	MC-65-64
R57	MC-65-66
R58	MC-65-68
R59	MC-65-69
R60	MC-65-70
R61	MC-50-10
R62	MC-50-11
R63	MC-50-12
R64	MC-50-13
R65	MC-50-14
R66	MC-94-09
R67	MC-94-10
R65	MC-94-11
R66	MC-94-12
R70	MC-94-14
R71	MC-94-15
R72	MC-94-16
R73	MC-94-18
R74	MC-94-19
R75	MC-94-20
R76	MC-94-21
R77	MC-94-23
R78	MC-94-27
R79	MC-94-25
R80	MC-94-26
R81	MC-94-27
R82	MC-94-28
R83	MC-94-29
R84	MC-94-30

Fleet number	Regn number
R85	MC-94-31
R86	MC-94-32
R87	MC-94-33
R88	MC-94-34
R89	MC-94-35
R90	MC-94-36
R91	MD 13-90
R92	MD-13-94
R93	MD-13-97
R94	MD-15-96
R95	MD-15-98
R96	MD-34-53
R97	MD-34-55
R98	MD-34-58
R99	MD-34-59
R100	MD-34-60
R101	MD-34-75
R102	MD-34-76
R103	MD-34-78
R104	MD-34-79
R105	MD-34-80
R106	MD-35-45
R107	MD-35-48
R108	MD-35-49
R109	MD-35-50
R110	MD-35-59
R111	MD-35-60
R112	MD-35-66
R113	MD-35-67
R114	MD-35-70
R115	MD-35-71
R116	MD-39-41
R117	MD-39-42
R118	MD-39-49
R119	MD-39-51
R120	MD-39-57
R121	MD-41-28
R122	MD-41-30
R123	MD-41-32
R124	MD-41-33
R125	MD-41-38
R126	MD-42-56
R127	MD-42-57
R128	MD-42-58
R129	MD 42-59
R130	MD-39-40
R131	MD-39-53
R132	MD-41-27
R133	MD-41-39
R134	MD-42-54
R135	MD 42-55
R136	MD-42-60
R137	MD-42-66
R138	MD-42-67
R139	MD-42-68
R140	MD-42-61
R141	MD 42-62
R142	MD-42-63
R143	MD-42-64
R144	MD-42-65
R145	MD-43-65
R146	ME-77-65
R147	ME-77-67
R145	ME-77-68
R149	ME-77-69
R150	ME-77-70
R151	ME-77-71
R152	ME 77-72
R153	ME-77-74
R154	ME-77-75
R155	ME-79-25
R156	ME-79-26
R157	ME-79-27
R158	ME-79-28
R159	ME-79-29
R160	ME-79-30
R161	ME-79-74
R162	MF-56-15
R163	MF-56-16
R164	MF-56-26
R165	MF-56-29
R166	MF-56-32
R167	MF-64-63
R168	MF-64-64
R169	MF-64-65
R170	MF-64-66
R171	MF-64-67

Fleet number	Regn number
R172	MF-64-71
R173	MF-64-73
R174	MF-64-75
R175	MF-64-82
R176	MF-64-83
R177	MF-64-84
R178	MF-64-85
R179	MF-64-86
R180	MF-64-91
R181	MF-64-92
R182	MF-64-98
R183	MF-64-99
R184	MF-65-00
R185	MF-65-01
R186	MF-65-04

Bristol K5G
(Tow Car)

Fleet number	Regn number
	M-10-73

Dennis Dart—

Chassis numbers all commence: 98SDL3060/

Fleet number	Regn number	Chassis number	Date to service
D 01	MF-77-09	/2952	02.01.96
D 02	MF-77-13	/2951	02.01.96
D 03	MF-77-14	/3034	02.01.96
D 04	MF-77-15	/2953	02.01.96
D 05	MF-77-16	/2954	02.01.96
D 06	MF-77-17	/2716	02.01.96
D 07	MF-77-18	/2950	02.01.96
D 08	MF-79-90	/3035	18.01.96
D 09	MF-80-01	/3037	18.01.96
D 10	MF-80-02	/3036	18.01.96

These chassis passed through Hong Kong on delivery. The first arrived in Hong Kong on 2nd December 1995 and the last was shipped to Macau on 25th december 1995. On average they spent about two days on Hong Kong soil.

The author thanks the PSV Circle for much of the fleet-list information on this page and Dennis Specialist Vehicles for late Dart data

The Buses of
TCM—Sociedade de Transportes de Colectivos de Macau, S.A.R.L.
澳門公共汽車有限公司

Following the 1988 reorganisation of Macau's bus operators, CTPEMI emerged under the new title 'Sociedade de Transportes de Colectivos de Macau, S.A.R.L.'—TCM—and took over some city bus routes as well as retaining its share of Route 11 to Taipa from the city. TCM is a joint venture with the Guangzhou Trolleybus Company.

The buses previously owned by CTPEMI, this included all the SB5 and VAS5 Bedfords but excluding the two small—B25F—Daihatsu midibuses, were absorbed and the fleet expanded to meet the new requirements of the expanded operation.

The first full-sized new buses were in the form of six Mercedes-Benz OF1313 single-deckers, made in Brasil, and eight similar sized Nissan UD CB12s. In addition a large fleet of Nissan Civilian minibuses was introduced.

Fleet numbers have been adopted and appear on most newer vehicles. By early 1996, the fleetname on buses had been altered to emphasise 'TCM' and 澳巴(AuBa—Macau Bus) in Chinese.

As the emphasis here is on British buses, it is of interest to learn that as 1995 turned into 1996, there remained a number of Bedford SB5's in daily service, including the first two from 1974, still in original condition, while others have been rebodied.

Bedford SB5—new to CTPEMI

The Bedford chassis has traditionally been regarded as a lightweight chassis in the UK and few have been subjected to heavy bus work over twenty or more years. In Macau, however, we have seen the Beadle-Bedfords of "Fok Lei" running under conditions undreamt of in rural Essex and we could see buses hurriedly purchased 'off the peg' in 1974, still in regular use into late 1995—a 21-year span operating less rigorous services than those to which the Beadles were subjected but still having to cope with very heavy loads. It is, therefore of added interest to learn that at least two of the 1974 batch were rebodied circa 1990 by Leun Shing. New, curved, windscreens were fitted and dual doorways were provided, both being

Vehicle Specification—Bedford SB5 - rebodied	
Chassis:	Bedford SB5
Engine:	Bedford 330 diesel
Gearbox:	David Brown 5-speed
Body:	Luen Shing
Body layout:	B51FdEXD,CEXD-OMO
Date rebodied:	c1990
Total:	3
Wheelbase:	18ft—5486mm
Weight:	10300kgs

within the wheelbase. All were withdrawn by January 1996, save MA-61-08, which was as a staff bus and two or three others which remained in a semi-derelict condition

BELOW: M-84-24 was new to CTPEMI in 1974 with Wong Ming single doorway bodywork and commenced work on the first bridge routes from Coloane and Taipa to Macau City. The robustness of the nominally lightweight chassis is obviously greater than previously accepted for, after years of heavy duty at least two of these chassis were rebodied by Luen Shing. Seen here laying over in 1995. *(Tim Phillips*

TOP LEFT: Wong Ming bodied Bedford SB5, M-83-29, of 1974, seen here in November 1995 carrying the livery of TCM who had numbered it L 02. This vehicle retained its single forward doorway and remained remarkably unaltered from its original condition. *(Tim Phillips*

LEFT: MA-61-09 was one of a pair of Bedford SB5's introduced by CTPEMI in 1980 with standard Wong Ming bodywork. When seen here in 1995, it had become L 12 in the TCM fleet but, apart from a change of colour, was largely unaltered. *(Tim Phillips*

LOWER LEFT: This deregistered Bedford VAS was new to CTPEMI in 1978 and had only recently been withdrawn when photographed in 1995. Apart from a change of livery and the application of fleet number L 11, this bus was relatively unchanged. *(Tim Phillips*

Mercedes-Benz OF1313

Soon after its formation in 1988, TCM took delivery of six Mercedes-Benz OF1313, front engined chassis with manual gearboxes and set-back front axles. These chassis were built by Mercedes-Benz do Brasil. SA.

Dual entrance bodywork was provided by Leun Shing, to a design that became the standard for future TCM buses and which bore a passing resemblance to the UABB bodies built for Fok Lei in the late 1970's.

RIGHT: This nearside view of TCM Mercedes-Benz 1313 (L 19) shows the similarity of the Leun Shing body design to that of the rebodied Bedford SB on page 92. The older style of red stripes and fleetname are carried. *(Timothy Phillips*

BELOW: Had it been carrying it, Mercedes-Benz MC-34-19 would have been fleet-numbered L 17. The AP1 route to the new Aeroporto is operated jointly with Transmac and for this service a number of 1313's were refurbished to run alongside new Transmac Dennis Darts. The simplified livery was adopted. *(Clement Lau*

Specification—Mercedes-Benz OF1313	
Chassis:	Mercedes-Benz OF1313
Engine:	Mercedes-Benz front mounted
Gearbox:	Mercedes-Benz manual
Body:	Leun Shing
Body layout:	B41FED,CXD-OMO
Total:	6

Mercedes-Benz OF1318

At the time of going to press, there were four rear-engined, Brasilian-built, Mercedes-Benz 0H1318 chassis in the course of being bodied in Hong Kong by Leun Shing with delivery to TCM due in February 1996. The OH.1318 chassis has a rear-mounted MB engine and power is transmitted by a fully automatic gearbox.

Fleet List—TCM vehicles inherited from CTPEMI

Bedford SB5

Fleet number	Regn number
L 01	M-83-27
L 02	M-83-29
L 03	M-84-24 #
L 04	M-84-25 #
L 05	M-84-71 #
L 06	M-84-73
L 07	M-85-39
L 08	M-85-40
L ?	MA-61-08
L 12	MA-61-09
L 13	MA-74-01
L 14	MA-74-02

Bedford VAS5

Fleet number	Regn number
L 11	MA-11-36
L 10	MA-11-37

Daihatsu

Fleet number	Regn number
Not used	M-98-34
Not used	M-98-35

\# Rebodied by Leung Shing   Note: Only MA-61-08 had any active role—as a staff bus—in late January 1996.

Fleet List—TCM 1996

Mercedes-Benz OF1313

Fleet number	Regn number
(15)	MC-34-06
(16)	MC-34-14
(17)	MC-34-19
(18)	MC-34-28
(19)	MC-34-57
L20	MC-34-98

Nissan CB12

Fleet number	Regn number
	MC-64-81
	MC-64-83
	MC-64-88
	MC-64-90
L27	MC-80-16
L28	MC-80-17
L29	MC-80-25
L30	MC-80-26

Nissan Civilian

Fleet number	Regn number	Fleet number	Regn number	Fleet number	Regn number	Fleet number	Regn number
S01	MC-17-12	S27	MC-60-64	S55	MD-25-00	S79	MD-33-03
S02	MC-17-26	S28	MC-60-65	S56	MD-25-01	S80	MD-33-04
S03	MC-17-77	S29	MC-60-67	S57	MD-25-02	S81	MD-33-05
S04	MC-17-92	S30	MC-60-69	S58	MD-25-03	S82	MD-33-06
S05	MC-18-01	S31	MC-62-07	S59	MD-25-04	S83	MD-33-07
S06	MC-18-02	S32	MC-62-09	S60	MD-25-05	S84	MD-33-09
S07	MC-18-04	S33	MC-62-12	S61	MD-25-09	S85	MD-33-10
S08	MC-18-05	S34	MC-62-13	S62	MD-25-12	S86	MD-33-12
S09	MC-18-08	S35	MC-62-18	S63	MD-25-14	S87	MD-32-14
S10	MC-18-32	S36	MC-62-20	S64	MD-25-16	S88	MD 33-15
S11	MC-18-49	S37	MC-62-21	S65	MD-32-79	S89	MD-33-16
S12	MC-18-85	S38	MC-62-27	S66	MD-32-80		MD-35-97
S13	MC-40-71	S39	MC-62-33	S67	MD-32-81		MD-35-99
S14	MC-40-75	S40	MC-75-76	S68	MD-32-85		MD-36-02
S15	MC-40-76	S41	MC-75-77	S69	MD-32-86		MD-36-05
S16	MC-40-77	S42	MC-75-78	S70	MD-32-87		MD-36-06
S17	MC-40-81	S43	MC-75-79	S71	MD-32-92		MD-36-08
S18	MC-40-85	S44	MC-75-80	S72	MD-32-93		MD-36-11
S19	MC-40-86	S45	MC-75-81	S73	MD-32-94		MD-36-12
S20	MC-40-87	S46	MC-75-82	S74	MD-32-95		MD-36-13
S21	MC-40-88	S47	MC-75-83	S75	MD-32-97		MD-36-16
S22	MC-40-89	S48	MC-75-84	S72	MD-32-93		MD-36-19
S23	MC-40-92	S49	MC-75-85	S73	MD-32-94		MD-36-20
S24	MC-40-94	S50	MC-75-86	S74	MD-32-95		MD-36-24
S25	MC-60-59	S51	MC-75-87	S75	MD 32-97		MD-36-27
S26	MC-60-63	S52	MC-75-89	S76	MD-32-98		
		S53	MC-75-90	S77	MD-33-01		
		S54	MC-75-91	S78	MD 33-02		

The author thanks the PSV Circle for much of the fleet-list information on this page

Nissan Diesel CB12 Citybus

In addition to the Mercedes-Benz, TCM also introduced eight front-engined buses built by Nissan Diesel Motor Co Ltd—as opposed to Nissan Motors, makers of the Civilian 'large mimibus'. These chassis, the CB12 'Citybus', have manual gearboxes and set-back front axles.

Bodywork supplied by Leun Shing was similar to that of the Mercedes-Benz referred to above and also had B41FE,CX-OMO arrangements.

Specification—Nissan CB12 Citybus

Chassis:	Nissan, Model CB12 'Citybus'
Engine:	Nissan
Gearbox:	Nissan
Body:	Leun Shing
Body layout:	B41FED,CXD-OMO
Total:	8

RIGHT: Another type, another nationality but the same basic body style as the Bedfords and Mercedes-Benz. Nissan UD Diesel CB12, No. L 29 seen late in 1995 heading for the border with China at Portas do Cerco on Route 10. *(Timothy Phillips*

Kee Kwan Motor Road Company

Established in order to provide cross-border transport, Kee Kwan Motor Road Company catered initially for passengers commuting between Macau and the local villages inside the People's Republic of China but, from 1980, has operated longer distance routes to more important destinations, including Guangzhou (Canton) about 140km to the north, Gahngsha and Guangmen. According to a 1980 newspaper report, the long distance service ran, at first at least, from the China side of the border gate but, by 1981 the service was extended to the Kee Kwan office in Macau, opposite the floating casino.

In the 1970's, Chinese vehicles routinely entered Macau but Macau vehicles rarely, if ever, entered China but, by the mid-1990's, visitors to Guangzhou could see the spectacle, unimaginable in the 1970's, of Hong Kong registered coaches parked alongside Macau registered vehicles in the forecourts of those major hotels that serve as termini for the long distance motor coach services now possible—many of those Macau coaches being from the fleet of Kee Kwan. It is reported to be only a matter of time before through road services will operate between Hong Kong and Macau.

Short distance cross-border shuttle services

During the 1973-76 period, the service of small Chinese-built buses from China into Macau was probably as little one or two journeys daily. As mentioned above, the vehicles used were small left-hand drive buses but with doors in the left side to suit them for left-hand rule of the road in Macau (*qv*). These came in two sizes; one approximating to today's midi-buses with about 30-seats and the other more like a minibus with possibly 16-seats. In addition, and somewhat surprisingly, British-built Commer minibuses were also used but, it is believed, they were never photographed.

By the time of the author's Christmas 1981 visit, these almost local routes were being operated on a very frequent headway from Kee Kwan's Macau terminal building, to destinations often only a short distance into China. Without actually checking the schedule, the frequency in late December 1981 appeared to be as often as five minute intervals at times. This is possibly a reflection on the size of vehicle that this operator preferred, their having about 30 seats.

The vehicles in evidence during 1981 were curious looking Isuzu single-deckers, very high framed, with boxy but modern-looking bodywork, the lowest step to the front entrance being at least two feet from the roadway. These buses were of right-hand-drive layout (China drives on the right; ie. left-hand-drive) with doorway located on the left-hand-side—standard Japanese and British domestic arrangement in fact. These vehicles were dual-registered with both Portuguese and Chinese (Guangdong)

licence plates. The licence numbers of Guangdong Province at that time being prefixed by the numbers 15 or 45.

Longer-distance midi-coaches

Kee Kwan's longer distance services between Macau and Guangzhou were operated by Isuzu 'Journey K' vehicles of that category that falls between minibus and a true midi—by 1990's standards— and whether these vehicles should be classified as 'large-mini's' or as 'small-midi's' is a moot point. Ke Kwan's version was a well appointed vehicle with a raised roof-line, air-conditioned and fitted with coach-style seats—plus a luggage pen behind the rearmost seats, all of which help to make this a comfortable long-distance conveyance. The body was painted in a metallic finish with broad bands of plain

ABOVE: In the 1970's, bus traffic between China and Macau was all Chinese operated and the vehicles were of Chinese origin, like this GF630, seen here in 1979. *(Ian Lynas*

BELOW: Kee Kwan Motor Road Company Isuzu high floor cross-border bus turns outside the company's office and terminal, opposite the Floating Casino in December 1981 *(Mike Davis*

colours along the roof-line and at waist level.

As these longer-distant Kee Kwan vehicles entered Macau solely to reach their terminal point, they were only registered in Guangdong, entering Macau on 'EX' series plates which are the Portuguese equivalent of the British Trade Plates and allow temporary use of this type of vehicle within Macau but between the terminal and border crossing.

Only local people holding either Chinese or Macau travel documents were permitted to enter China by way of Kee Kwan's buses; both foreign tourists and non-Chinese residents of Macau being required to enter the PRC in an organized 'closed-door' tour-group which both started and finished in Macau.

The 1990's

In the 1990's, Kee Kwan uses Nissan R85HXRs and RM81HXRs with Fuji bodies and Isuzus with Wong Ming bodies on its cross-border shuttle service. Kee Kwan also uses coaches of international standard, Japanese in origin and operates services from Macau to local Chinese destinations:

ABOVE: Longer distance routes commenced in 1980 from the China side of the border gate but by December 1981 these had been extended into Macau as seen here near the "Fok Lei" bus station. This Isuzu 'Journey K' was fitted with a Macau-style temporary registration as it entered the territory, it being removed as the vehicle departed Portuguese jurisdiction en route for Guangzhou then still popularly known outside China as Canton. *(Mike Davis*

BELOW: A sister vehicle stands outside the Kee Kwan offices in Macau having just arrived from China. *(Mike Davis*

Kee Kwan operats from Macau to:-

珠海	Zhu Hai
中山	Zong Shan
順德	Shun De
番禺	Pan Yu
佛山	Fo Shan
西樵	Xi Qiao
肇慶	Zhaq Qing
廣州	Guang Zhou
清縣	Quing Yuan

Other British Passenger Vehicles in the 1970's & 80's

Most independant operators in Macau during the 1970's were small and only owned one or two vehicles which were predominately British in origin with Ford, Austin, Bedford Commer, Karrier, Morris, and Seddon being represented. There was a sprinkling of Japanese and German vehicles in evidence but British makes had been readily obtainable on the second-hand market from Hong Kong. Changing attitudes and circumstances eroded the 'Buy British' tradition and the early 1980's saw Japanese makes sweep into Macau.

A number of British Fords and Bedfords graced the streets well into the 1980'sbut the products of Nissan, Isuzu, stc. became the norm, particularly after General Motors made Isuzu its regional product over Bedford. The first two second-hand Japanese coaches arrived in early 1978, from which time the British interest has declined.

Bodywork on non-integral vehicles of all origins continues in the 1990's, with a decidedly Hong Kong flavour but many Japanese units come as completely-built-up, factory-produced, standard vehicles such as have become commonplace throughout Asia.

In addititon the more comfortably appointed tourist vehicle, some schools and factories operate their own transport, often using lorry or van-derived models. All sizes of vehicle are to be seen from the common 14-seats minibus through midibuses to the full size coach with 36 or more seats.

In 1974 the remains of a Bedford OB were discovered on the City rubbish dump. The derelict vehicle had the shell of a British-built body, possible by Mulliner. The right-hand-drive chassis carried the number OB26532 while the engine number was OB29782. The history of this vehicle may be interesting.

With more liberal views taking hold in China, tourist traffic developed during the 1980's and quite early in the decade there were a number of coaches based in Macau that carried sightseeing parties relatively short distances inside the People's Republic. However, with the demise of the British coach chassis, there is little likelyhood that British made coaches will again grace the streets of Macau whilst in the ownership of a Macanese operator. But then, again, Dennis broke into the Macau bus market......

LEFT: M94-06—the first hyphen was missing from the registration— was a Ford Thames Trader 4D; a chassis similar to those of Kowloon Motor Bus AD4713, etc. It was photographed in 1976 with Taipa Island as a backdrop and is believed to have been in the service of a technical college. *(Derek Lucas*

RIGHT: M-10-64 was a little Austin owned by the Macau Department of Tourism—S.T.D.M.—and had about 16-seats. It was seen here in 1976 but with the opening-up of Macau to world tourism during the 1970's, standards of comfort quickly improved, leaving this attractive, but spartan, bus behind. *(Derek Lucas*

ABOVE: M-73-69 was a Seddon RE, similar to a number sold to operators in Hong Kong and was working for Hi-No-De-Caravela Tours when photographed in 1976. (Author's collection

RIGHT: Sister vehicle, M-73-70 seen from the rear, showing the rear engine and vents. (John Shearman

BELOW: This smart airconditioned Commer, M-10-13, was to be seen in the mid-1970's working for Estoril Tours.

LEFT: A publicity photograph by Wallace Harper, the Hong Kong Ford agents and importers of British Aluminium body kits. This Ford R192 is very representative of the type in Macau. This vehicle was the property of the Macau Jai-Alai Co. Ltd. *(John Shearman collection*

CENTRE LEFT: An impressive 1982 line-up of Ford coaches belonging to Estoril Tours who operated from the forecourt of the Lisboa Hotel. *(Mike Davis*

LEFT: Two more Fords, with the opposition creeping-in on the right! *(Mike Davis*

Bus Tickets

The bus tickets issued by Companhia de Auto-Carros "Fok Lei" Ltda and those of the Auto-Carros de Taipa were similar in style, being 'geographical', showing termini; those of "Fok Lei" showed six points. On no journey made by either John Shearman or the author, was a ticket issued on a Coloane island bus of Lo Wan Lee On bus company. After their takeover, however, CTPEMI issued tickets on all services, intra-island, inter-island and, later, cross-bridge.

With a minor exception, all tickets were printed on flimsy, glazed paper that was, semi-waterproof; the latter being essential to protect the blocks of tickets clutched in the hand of the conductress, often in very hot and humid conditions, inside an oven like metal bus.

The exception was a type of ticket printed on thin brown wrapping paper at such times as when the correct type of paper was temporarily unavailable. This was also used by CTPEMI on all journeys made by the author.

Tickets were printed in Macau in a secure upstairs room over a paper-goods shop while the flimsy paper was of Chinese origin.

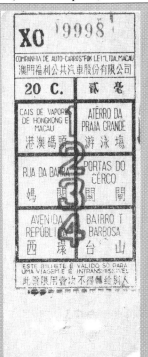

LEFT: Tickets kindly lent by Ron Phillips, showing two denominations as issued by Auto-Carros "Fok Lei" prior to the fare increase in October 1974.

RIGHT: After the fares increase, the size of "Fok Lei" tickets was reduced (the basic adult fare rose from 20c (Avos) to 30c and new fares were introduced for the cross-bridge routes, Macau to Taipa being 1 Pataca ($) and Macau to Coloane 1.50 Patacas. The three tickets illustrated above show "Fok Lei" tickets. The centre, $1 ticket, FT 9386 was kindly lent by John Shearman whilst the remainder in the smaller format are from the authors's collection. (All tickets shown here are actual size.)

7GZ 5045: By 1982, the fare structure had again been altered and the minimum city fare for an adult was 50c.

5A 003329: The equivalent $1 CTPEMI ticket issued for journeys between Macau and Taipa, printed on brown paper.

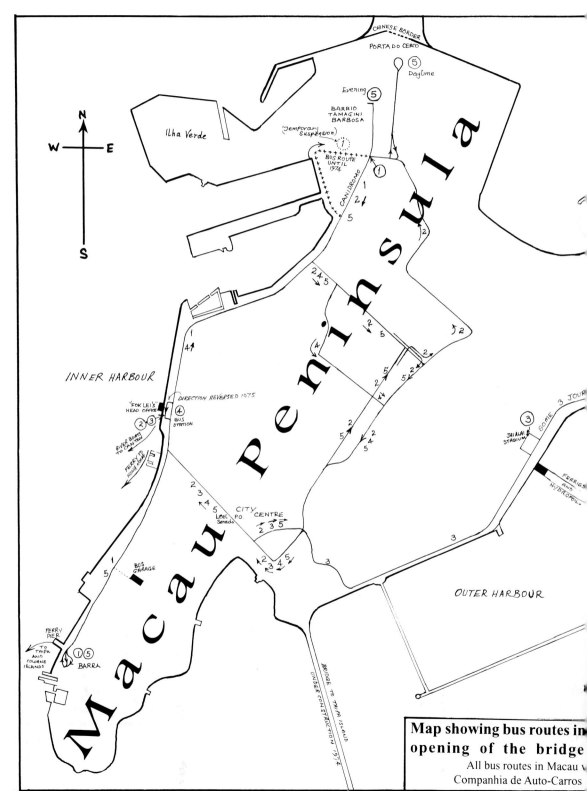

CHINESE BORDER

PORTA DO CERCO

⑤ Daytime

Evening ⑤

BARRIO TAMAGINI BARBOSA

Ilha Verde

(Temporary Suspension) ①

BUS ROUTE UNTIL 1974

CANIDROMO

①

1
2
5

2

2 A 5

2
5

2

2

1
A

2
5

2
5

2
5

INNER HARBOUR

'FOK LEI'S' HEAD OFFICE

DIRECTION REVERSED 1975

② ③
④ BUS STATION

RIVER BOATS TO CANTON

FERRY TO HONG KONG

2 3 4 5
Leal Senado

CITY P.O. CENTRE

2 3 5

2 3 4 5

③ JAI ALAI STADIUM

SOME 3 JOUR

FERRIES AND HYDROFOIL

3

BUS GARAGE

5

OUTER HARBOUR

FERRY PIER

TO TAIPA AND COLOANE ISLANDS

① ⑤ BARRA

3

BRIDGE TO TAIPA ISLAND

UNDER CONSTRUCTION 1974

Macau Peninsula

Map showing bus routes in
opening of the bridge

All bus routes in Macau v
Companhia de Auto-Carros

4, just before the
Taipa Island.

perated by
Lei" Limitada

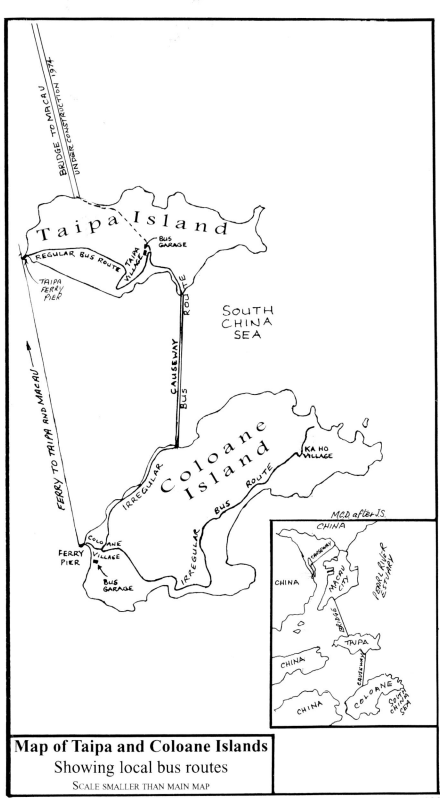

Map of Taipa and Coloane Islands
Showing local bus routes
SCALE SMALLER THAN MAIN MAP

Fok Lei Service Vehicles

In 1973/4, Companhia de Auto-Carros "Fok Lei" Ltda had a small fleet of service cars, comprising a small Bedford lorry with war-time-style bonnet assembly, registered M-10-73, an Austin 'Loadstar' lorry, M-34-64, and a Bristol L5G converted from a bus and more fully described on page 22. Both the Bedford and Austin were second-hand from the British military, purchased at auction in Hong Kong.

When it became necessary to replace the Austin 'Loadstar' lorry in 1977, one of the Beadle-Bedford buses was taken from a line awaiting the scrap-man and was reconstructed as an open-backed lorry. The Austin's registration was transferred to the 'Beadle lorry'.

There is some doubt about the fate of L104X, the shortened Bristol L5G with the chassis believed to have been 48.052. The facts are that about 1981, a totally rebuilt Bristol L5G breakdown crane appeared with registration M-12-09, followed by another registered M-10-73, taken from the Bedford lorry.

One possibility is: the original M-12-09 was in need of a major overhaul and to replace it another L5G was rebuilt as a short-wheelbase breakdown crane. When the original M-12-09 (48.052) was taken off the road, that registration number was transferred to the 'new' vehicle; the 'old' vehicle—48.052—was taken into workshops and refurbished and given a new body. It received the transferred registration M-10-73 taken from the Bedford lorry. On the other hand, they might both have been newly converted chassis and the original L104x was scrapped. The answer may now never be known.

TOP: The ex-military Bedford lorry, M-10-73 seen at the bus station in 1974. *(John Shearman*

ABOVE: Also ex-military, from Hong Kong, was Austin 'Loadstar', M-34-64 photographed outside the "Fok Lei" yard that was then still its only depot, near the Barra terminus in 1975. *(Mike Davis*

BELOW LEFT: Bristol L5G breakdown lorry, M-12-09, photographed in 1983. *(Mike Davis* **BELOW RIGHT:** The second of the 'new' breakdown trucks, M-10-73, that had been converted from buses. *(John Shearman — But, which is the new one?*